MAN UP!

A PRACTICAL GUIDE TO BEING A DAD

Dennis A. Daniel

Published by SOS Publishing, with Next Century Publishing, www.NextCenturyPublishing.com

Printed in the United States of America

ISBN: 978-1939-268-167

To reach the author:

www.manupthebook.com

For us Dads, nothing comes close to the thrill, the joy, and the peace ... of being a great Dad.

Contents

Acknowledgments

This book stems from the relationships with the most important people in my life; my parents, my wife and my kids. My parents helped to shape me into the person that I am, through both nature and nurture. I learned the tough side of being a Dad from my father and I learned the soft side of being a Dad from my mother.

My wife has put up with my presence and absences, my happy times and tirades, my strengths and weaknesses, my imperfections and reparations for over 30 years.

Through it all, we have grown together, loved each other and supported each other. I owe her everything.

My kids ... are the best kids any father could ask for. They are loving people like their Mom. They are hardworking, strong and opinionated like their Dad. They are forgiving of both their Mother and me. They are the kind of people that the world needs more of and they are just starting families of their own. I am writing this book in thanks for them and to share with them a few things that they will, hopefully, see fit to pass on to their kids.

Introduction

Last year, my wife and I experienced the weddings of our first two children. For years, we wondered if they would find the right people. We wondered if they were too picky. We wondered if they were living in the right area to find "the right ones." We wondered if we would ever have grandkids. When we spoke with them over the phone, we wanted to know who they were dating, how it was going, and if they were visiting the right places to meet the right people.

I don't know if this is typical or not, but my wife and I are both from smaller towns. We married at 20, and have been together for over 30 years. Our parents married young, and had each been married to the same person, for over 45 and 50 years respectively. In short, we came from a long line of dinosaurs. In today's age, kids wait longer to get married, they wait longer to have children, have fewer children and frankly, the likelihood of long lasting relationships is becoming more and more rare.

All of this was weighing on our minds as we tried to be patient and supportive as our oldest two children grew through their mid 20's searching for their life mates.

Then, each child met a wonderful person and, within the space of a few months, we went from no weddings to two. It was at these weddings that the first kernel of this book began to take shape. Over the two wedding weekends, my wife and I were both repeatedly told what great people our children were. Frankly, to us they were just our kids. But to everyone else, they were clearly different. They were somehow special. I can't tell you how many times we were told, "I wish that I knew your secret to parenting, because it certainly worked on them" or "You should bottle your parenting skills" or "You should write a book."

I found myself over the next few months, trying to figure out what was so special about our kids and what was special about the way they were raised. I started to realize that I had a bunch of little snippets, anecdotes or philosophies that were simple, direct, repeatable and distinctly different than many parents used. I often found myself sharing these anecdotes with young men starting their families and they seemed to resonate.

A friend of mine asked me a few months later, "What is the one great work of your life?" I answered without skipping a beat, "Being a Dad — it exudes from my very being. I knew from the time that I was a small kid, that I was called to be a Dad. I could feel it in my bones. I am a Dad at home, I am a Dad at work, heck, even my initials are DAD."

Shortly after this conversation, I found myself out of work and for the first time in 38 years, I actually had time on my hands. After several months of standard job seeking (we'll talk about Dad's job in a later chapter), I started to think more and more of the conversation about my "great work in life."

I realized that I had spent a whole lot of time on my career, but not a lot of time on what I considered to be my "great calling." After a few months, I started to think that maybe I was being called to write this book so that others could benefit from what I have learned. You see, I believe that there is a great deal of lost wisdom. There are things that have been lost in the world of psychotherapists and child psychologists. There are things lost to the "ME" generation. There are things lost to the multiple attempts at improving kids "self-esteem."

There is a great deal that we can learn from looking at successful parents, looking at successful marriages and the fact that children benefit when they have a mother and a father who are doing their best to raise a family.

All too often, kids today are reared by a mother and an absent father. She is doing the best she can, but she is only half of the equation. Well guys, it is time for us to MAN UP! It is time to share and to learn some simple guidelines on becoming successful Dads. And believe me, after practicing these guidelines, you will get more out of the love of a child than you will ever receive from your work, your extracurricular activities or your money.

I am not a PhD, nor a professional counselor, nor a certified expert. I am proud to say that I am just a Dad. In these few pages, I have tried to capture a way of life that has worked for us and has yielded three terrific kids. I hope that my lessons learned and advice will help you to raise wonderful kids and strengthen your families as well.

MANSPEAK

To set the tone of this book, I am not about to pull any punches. Frankly, we are too politically correct, and as a result, we aren't getting the full effect of the wisdom from the past. So, I am going to write the book just like men need to hear it. There will be some funny stuff, (at least to me), some stories and some serious stuff. There will be a little religion. This will be written just like guys need to hear it. It will be up front and to the point. A little like the talk on a weekend with the boys.

To begin with, let's put the cards on the table. For the better part of the last 50 years, men have been mocked as a bunch of losers. Look at the men on TV. Men are most often portrayed as: idiots, effeminate, crooks, sex fiends, or some combination, thereof. Even the good guys are only successful when they beat up or kill someone else.

Men that used to be role models have been chastened for impurity, and sports figures have gone from guys like Palmer to characters like Tiger. Politicians pull stunts that most guys could never get away with and society just looks the other way.

The economics of "we want it all right now," have made it nearly impossible to raise a family on a single income. As a result, both parents are working and the kids are often on the loose. Fathers regularly promote abortion or father a child, then leave. They marry one woman, divorce, marry another and so on. Fathers abdicate their responsibility to the Mom, the school or the police. This is a rampant problem, not just in America but worldwide.

To quote a famous philosopher, Pogo, "We have found the enemy and he is us." Guys, we are screwing things up, and the only way for this to get turned around is for us to MAN UP and start to shoulder our responsibilities as Dads. I use the term Dad, because any moron can father a child, but it takes a Dad to raise one. This book is all about keys to being a Dad.

We are the best-educated people that the world has ever known. Yet in the one area that is most important, collectively, we stink. Look at it like this; when you build a structure, everyone knows that you build a solid foundation, then frame up the walls, put a roof on it, then fill in the details and build it out for comfort.

If you look at how humanity has evolved, it started with the family as the foundation, next came the tribe, the locality, the nation and finally the world-wide system. **But, the foundational element is the family.** The family is the basic building block of society. If the family is weak, then society will be weak. Well boys, if you look around you, every data point out there shows that the family is weak. The divorce rate, the abortion rate, the birth rate, the infidelity rate are all problematic.

Even the definition of the family itself is being attacked. C'mon guys, be reasonable. If the family didn't consist of a male and a female, we wouldn't even exist. REPRODUCTION CAN'T OCCUR WITHOUT A MAN AND A WOMAN! Just because we can redefine, doesn't mean it is the right thing to do.

Now I know I just bent a lot of folks out of shape, but this is what I mean by man-speak. We have to get it on the table, rationalize where we are and move forward if we are going to do the job we are called to do as men. Now I promise that I am not going to be bashing people throughout this book, but I am going to raise issues that need to be addressed. You have to decide if you want to hear it and whether or not you are going to do something with it.

As I said earlier, I am not worried about political correctness, this topic is just too important. The fundamental structure of humanity is in a terrible state of disrepair, but all you hear about on the news is the economy, or politics, or Wall Street or war. No one talks about the state of the family. Trying to resolve these other issues without strengthening the family is like re-spackling the walls without addressing a cracked foundation. It might look ok for a while, but the next crack that shows up will be a lot worse and eventually the house will just crumble.

One more thing on man-speak: for good Dads, everything you read in this book will seem like common sense. This book will be more like a summary or a refresher to what you are doing well. A lot about being a Dad is just using good old common sense.

Well boys, the problem is that common sense ain't so common anymore. This book is about sharing things that some men take for granted but that other men may see as enlightening. As you read through these pointers and tips, just ask yourself, "Does this make sense?" If it does, then follow it. It is a simple recipe for being a successful Dad.

Guys, the fundamental family structure is under attack. If we don't MAN UP and fix it, our society is in deep trouble. This book is all about helping other men shore up the foundations of our families.

MAN UP Memos

- ✔ The family is the foundation of society.
- ✔ The state of the modern family is in disrepair.
- ✔ Men must help repair the foundation of society.

Disclaimer, We Screwed Up

For every successive generation, since about 1200 AD, each generation has been able to better the last. In this country, at least, every generation since we were founded has been able to surpass the last in standard of living and economic improvement.

My parents and grandparents saw the introduction of electricity, running water and extensive human flight. In the span of my grandfather's lifetime, we went from farming via horse drawn plow to landing men on the moon.

My parent's generation, called "the Greatest Generation", tried to give their children all of the benefits they could. My generation is the first, for many families, where a college education was the norm rather than a privilege of the few. My generation has seen the explosion of the information age and an economic boom like none other in world history.

In spite of these economic and social advancements, when it comes to our family life, the results are startlingly disquieting. Our birth rate is less than replenishment. Nearly 50 percent of all marriages end in divorce. There have been over 50 million babies aborted in this nation alone since 1974. Schools can no longer discipline kids and kids are out of control. There is a rampant drug problem, and STD's have hit the highest level since the introduction of penicillin.

So what went wrong? Well guys ... We screwed up. In my opinion, my generation took advantage of all the things our parents tried to do for us and blew it. We turned into a huge bunch of spoiled brats. We wanted it "Our Way," and if it didn't suit us then we protested. In other words, "I'll just pick up my toys and go home." What is worse is that this is the mentality we have passed on to our children!

We have failed to instill the discipline of respect, of hard work, of playing by the rules and of living with the consequences of the decisions that we make. We teach kids that everyone gets a trophy if they contributed or not. We teach kids that if they whine about it long enough Mommy and Daddy will cave in and they can have what they want. We teach kids that just like on the computer game, if you fail to reach the next level, just hit restart and the game starts all over again.

The problem is that this isn't how life works. If we don't prepare our kids to work, to respect, to play by the rules, they are going to have their butts handed to them when it comes to life. They are going to be out-hustled by every new wave of immigrants that come to this nation. They are going to fall by the wayside and end up wondering why they can't find anything more meaningful to do than flip burgers, while their peers from India, Asia, Latin America, Africa, and Persia, work circles around them. If you don't think it's true, here are a couple of anecdotal data points.

A few years ago I was having lunch with two co-workers who happened to be from India. Raj held two advanced degrees, worked 80 hours per week for a Fortune 500 company, was a self-taught expert in a number of fields, owned several personal businesses, all of which were very successful. In short, he was one of the most brilliant hard-working people I have ever met. Sri was a very good industrial engineer, (better than average according to American standards) was married, lived debt free and was a good "American level " worker.

While at lunch, I asked each of them to explain why they came to this country. Raj said that he had had a falling out with his family and he had come to America because of the freedom to succeed. Raj explained how he was taking advantage of all of the opportunities that such a great country offered.

Sri expressed, "Look, we both know Raj and how exceptional he is." "Realistically, we both know that I do not possess his skills, his intellect or his drive, but I do consider myself a very good industrial engineer. In America, I compete very well against American workers. I can raise a family, make a good income and do well here." He continued, "In America, I do not fear the competition because here, I only have one Raj to compete against and the rest are just typical Americans. But in India, I cannot compete. Rather than one Raj per company, there are hundreds of guys like Raj, and I would be competing against all of them for every job out there!"

Here is one more story to bring the point home. A few years ago, I was asked to speak at a Masters in Industrial Engineering Program at Texas A&M University. I was surprised that, out of a class of about a hundred very bright students, there was only one student who was a native-born American! Every other student in the class was from another country, attending a top flight American university, learning from the best professors in the world, and working their tails off to get ahead. And there was ONE NATIVE-BORN AMERICAN OUT OF ONE HUNDRED STUDENTS!

Guys, here's the deal: my generation screwed up. We focused on everything but the family and now our children are not prepared to compete in the marketplace as it looms ahead. We had it our way and now our kids are unprepared to raise families with the right level of respect, work ethic and drive. The fact is that there are literally billions of very capable people from all over this planet that can get a visa, hop on a plane and be here with a totally different mindset and skill-set. That fact has the potential of putting American children in the passenger seat.

On the watch of my generation, we collectively failed the family test. In the meantime, the world has gotten a lot smaller, a lot more competitive and our sons and daughters have their backs up against a wall whether they realize it or not. And what's worse is that we haven't left them a legacy of how to teach their own kids the right way to build that fundamental building block of society.

Boys, the world is changing. In a global world, our kids have to compete against the best. Our family structure is the foundation that raises successful kids. And right now, a large number of our families are in disrepair. As men, we have to get back to shouldering our responsibility for our families or our kids and grandkids will suffer the consequences. It's just that simple.

MAN UP Memos

- ✔ The family has suffered as a result of the Baby Boom.
- ✔ The world will challenge our children and grandchildren.
- ✔ Men today must re-learn to be Good Dads.

Why I Wrote This Book

First of all, I am not the perfect Dad. I have screwed up countless times. And, if you don't believe that, just ask my wife and kids. But, I do consider myself to be a better than average Dad. As I mentioned earlier, I have three kids that have turned out to be successful, competent, happy individuals. Fortunately, all of my kids hope to have their own families.

My wife and I have done all we can to impart some wisdom to our children. They have learned through the way we have raised them and from the countless conversations about our philosophy. We have passed on the things we have learned from our parents, the things that have worked and the things that haven't worked.

We now have the opportunity to share parenting tips with our daughter-in-law and son-in-law. They are each the products of their own families and come with their own parenting philosophies. But the common denominator is that all of our children want to improve on the things that they have learned.

If you think about it, evolution occurs in pretty much everything. You can see it in the patterns in nature and you can see it in the behavioral pattern of people. I am a firm believer that each generation of parents really tries to do it a little better than the generation before.

So the first reason that I am writing this book is as a gift to my children and grandchildren. My children have always been willing to learn from others and I am hoping that I can impart a little more wisdom, so they can do it better for their kids than I did for them.

I guess it is a little bit of the theory of evolution. Each generation tries to improve on the last. My folks tried to do a better job than theirs and I am trying to do a better job than my folks did. I have heard so many times, "Too bad there isn't an owner's manual that comes with your first kid!" I guess that this is a start on that owner's manual. From a Dad's perspective, I want to give my children an edge on some things they can learn.

The second reason I am writing this book is there are so many young men out there who are fathering children that have absolutely no clue what they are doing. It is not necessarily their fault; they just haven't had good role models from which to learn.

There aren't any classes called "Being a Dad." Many of these young men haven't had a good Dad to teach them. They are not prepared with what to do, how to do it or what they should be doing. We teach them about sex education, but not how to positively deal with the consequences. And, we definitely do not teach them how to MAN UP and be a real Dad! This book is for them. I am hoping that some small percentage will pick up this book, read it and learn from it. Maybe a few will give it to their friends, or their brothers.

Finally, I am writing this book for the unsung heroes, the rank and file of the great Dads out there. The guys who are doing it right, who love their kids and raise them the right way, the ones who sacrifice their lives and their energy to provide for their families. The Dads who coach, teach and mentor their own kids and the children of others. The Dads who cradle the newborn and bury the son that has gone to war, because of what his Dad has taught him.

Somehow, the good Dads out there have to spread the wealth. We have to help the next generation succeed. As I said before, "My generation screwed up," so my generation needs to help solve the problem. This is my small part. Maybe this book will spawn a new generation of Dads. Maybe it will just help one guy be a better Dad. If this book helps one Dad then it is worth every minute. If this book is just a gift to my own family, then it is worth every minute as well.

MAN UP Memos

- ✔ All generations want to improve on the last.
- ✔ This book is about sharing wisdom.
- ✔ This book is for men who didn't have a good role model.
- ✔ This book is to celebrate great Dads everywhere.

PHILOSOPHY

One of the most eventful conversations that I ever had was on my very first date with my wife. In fact, it wasn't really even a date. She and her folks had come to my hometown and had stopped by to visit my parents, as they had been friends for years. At the time, my wife and I had not seen each other since we were infants, but I thought it would be a great idea for me to show her around town (especially since she was so cute.)

To make a long story short, we sat on the front porch of her sister's house talking till the wee hours of the night. We spoke about everything! In particular, we talked about the type of marriage each of us wanted to have. We talked about the way we wanted to raise our kids. Now, having this sort of an in-depth conversation on the first night we had ever met probably seems a little over the top. But for us, on that night, it was just a natural conversation.

We were able to share our philosophies and what was so unusual is that our philosophies aligned. What became even more important is, once we knew we were right for each other, we were willing to live out those philosophies in the way our children were raised and the way we lived our lives.

Gentlemen, you did not father that child by yourselves. It takes two to make a child and it takes two to rear one. The only way to be successful in raising a child is when you and Mommy share the same philosophy.

Family life is tough. Living with a number of people that depend upon your decision-making, your ability to earn an income, your consistency and discipline is challenging in the best of times. If you and Mommy do not agree philosophically on just about everything, you are in deep trouble. The two of you have to be aligned. You cannot be debating with each other when there are kids watching the outcome.

The day you first marry will be a life-changing event, as the two of you now have to work as a team. When that first little one comes, you will have to tag team just to keep up with that squirming little ball of energy and poop and it will stress you to the max. When number two comes, you have to learn man-to-man coverage. This is still pretty stressful, but manageable if you are working with the same philosophy. By the time number three or four come along, you have to play zone defense. You had better understand the positions, because they outnumber you and you can lose the game.

The two of you have to be aligned on everything from the number of kids to the manner in which they are disciplined and from the way you budget to the way that you will share family time. Listen up ... you are not the ruler of the family; you are an equal and complementary partner to your wife. The two of you have to agree on which decisions belong to Mom, which ones belong to Dad and which ones are joint decisions.

Debating this within earshot of the kids is not a good idea. They WILL divide and conquer and they WILL use one of you against the other. I don't know where this "deviousness" comes from, but it is there and they use it masterfully from a very early age. The point is, when you see a division in opinion coming, call time out, get with your wife, discuss the next play and then get back in the game.

In my opinion, the best time to get philosophically aligned is before you ever become engaged. If you can't get aligned philosophically, you probably aren't the right fit, so move on. The next best time to align is before you start having kids. This gives you a chance to get things aligned before the battle joins. But for gosh sakes, as a worst case, take the time to talk and get on the same page before the kids are old enough to eavesdrop and know how to use divisions against you!

Once you have learned how to talk and align ... keep it up. As the kids grow, they will continuously come up with new and challenging offenses. You and your wife have to stay a step ahead or they will run amok. If you and your wife can't control a two year old, then you don't stand a chance when the little booger picker is a teenager.

When the two of you came together and created them, you signed up for the responsibility to raise them, as well. Make sure that you get aligned on a philosophy that gives you the best chance to succeed and gives your child the best chance to become a happy and productive adult.

MAN UP Memos

- ✔ Successful parenting requires alignment between parents.
- ✔ Kids will divide and conquer if you are not aligned.
- ✔ Get aligned before engaging tough issues with your kids.
- ✔ If you can't control a two year old, you don't stand a chance with a teenager.

It's Not the Economy, Stupid!

If you read the book of Genesis, the very first commandment that God ever gave to man was, "Go forth, be fruitful, multiply and subdue the earth." This very first statement sets up, not only our role but also the priority of what we are supposed to do.

Notice: God did not say, "Go find a job, build a career, buy a bunch of expensive toys and when you are financially able, go have 2.1 kids per household." God did not say, "I will only send you kids when you want them and oh, by the way, if you get pregnant and you aren't happy about it, just reverse the call and kill the baby. It is just a collection of cell tissue until it miraculously pops out."

With the command to go forth and multiply, He basically says, go start your family. Get your job, trust in Him and He will help take care of things. Here is an astonishing fact; people have pretty much followed God's first command for 100,000 years and have done pretty well.

It is just in the last 60 years or so that we figured out "The Pill," legalized abortion and that "Miller time first and family last" is what life is all about. Over the last 60 years, we have collectively put job, career, cool toys, a bank account, housing and everything else ahead of family. And oh, by the way, as a result of this new and improved mindset; divorce is up, single parent families are up, abortion has skyrocketed, drug use is rampant, STD's are up, mental illness is up ... you get the picture. When we started putting family life last, we screwed up society.

Here's an alert for you. Who is going to keep the economy going if there aren't young people to backfill the retirees? Hint, hint, either the population implodes and there aren't enough folks to keep an economy going or there is a huge economic vacuum and it is backfilled by immigrants.

Here's another alert. Demographers have noted that based on the current birthrates, Europe and China are each about to undergo population implosions, on the order of 40 to 50% population shrinkage over the next 40 years. How's that gonna work for their economic systems?

Another interesting fact is that the only thing growing the American population right now is the influx of immigrants. So what does that mean for the U.S.? It is the same song, just a different verse. If it weren't for the opportunity to succeed in America, drawing immigrants from all over the world, we would be doomed to the same fate as Europe. This is the legacy that we have left our children. Now you might say, "No problem, the U.S. has always been a melting pot." My answer is, "Yes, it has and the pot is about to melt all over again."

Is this really a problem? Well, on an historic scale, probably not. Migration has always been there, cultures have grown, morphed and died; but there is another level to consider. With each family having, on average, around two kids, that means that if you are lucky, you may have one son. If he goes on to father a boy, maybe your family lives on for another generation.

In my case, my grandfather's family name died with his generation. No male heirs. Out of my personal family, there were five kids, I was the only one to have children and of our three kids, there is only one boy. So my son is the only one able to extend my family name. Either he has a son or my family name dies with his generation. This pattern is repeating itself all across America.

Now, you may not think much about it when you are 35 and just thinking of settling down. But, when you are 60 and there ain't no more kids coming, you will be wondering how your legacy will live on. If you haven't noticed, there are very few men whose names are remembered three weeks after they are gone (like, maybe Elvis). The only thing that provides a real legacy is our children and their children. Without them, there is no legacy. This is just a little something to think about while doing your family planning.

Now does that mean you have to have a litter of kids? No, it doesn't. It just means make sure that you aren't putting more emphasis on the economics than is due. Have a little faith that if you happen to be blessed with kids, God will also help you to provide for them. He took care of our ancestors for 100,000 years. If you ask, He'll probably take care of you too!

MAN UP Memos

- ✔ Family is more important than money and cool toys.
- ✔ Reproduction rate is less than population replacement.
- ✔ Your legacy comes from your children.
- ✔ Consider all of this when family planning.

BEING A DAD

A few months ago, I was in a men's group at church, and the speaker was talking about what it means to be a Father. He quoted from the creation story in Genesis and summarized it like this. The first thing God did for man was to bring him into creation. The second thing God did was to try to bring man joy. This is what being a real Father or "Dad" is all about. Create life first; then, try to bring your children joy. Biologically speaking, through the gift of the father and the receptiveness of the mother, a new child is created. After that, a real Dad will spend his entire life trying to bring joy to his children.

This is the model that we are called to emulate as Dads. It is as simple as that and every good Dad, regardless of the culture, does their best to follow that pattern. Now a lot of you may be calling for the BS card but I want to explain further. No real Dad ever wants ill for his children.

A child may look at the rules and think, "Dad's rules sure don't make me very happy! There ain't no joy in them rules!" But the fact is that children do not have the wisdom to set the rules nor do they have the experience to know what is safe and what isn't. Everyone goes through this. It is just part of our nature.

My siblings used to get upset about my Dad's rules. We all thought that our old man was over the top on rules and that we were held to a tighter set of restrictions than "everybody else." My Dad's philosophy was pretty much, "If you live under my roof, then you live by my rules." To my siblings (and most kids) this seemed "totally unfair." To me, it seemed pretty straightforward and logical.

Dad once told me a story from in the 1930's, when his family horse went lame. He and his brother were strapped to the plow and had to pull the plow in order to get the crop sowed. It wasn't out of animosity from his old man. It was out of necessity. So getting back to Dad's rules, I kind of looked at them from a different perspective.My Dad never made me pull a plow so I figured that the rest of Dad's rules weren't too bad. Looking back, I realize that every rule that I had either taught me how to survive or helped to keep me safe and out of trouble. I didn't know it at the time but Dad's rules were there because he loved me.

You can look at the Ten Commandments the same way. Now a lot of you may be thinking, "There he goes, getting all religious on us," but let me explain. If you think about it, the Ten Commandments are pretty solid rules that allow mankind to run a society. They set boundary conditions that we operate within. We are free to operate within the boundaries and no one gets hurt, as long as everyone plays by the rules.

It is no different than football or baseball. Someone sets the rules so everyone can play and enjoy the game. The Ten Commandments are just the rules for the game of life. If everyone lives by the rules then we can all play and have a good time. The fact is, that pretty much every society accepts and follows the same rules, and the only time that there are issues is when people or countries break the rules. The rules are there for our own good.

By following the rules and living our lives within them, we are taught how to live lives with Joy. For the believer, God planted the seeds of these rules in the human psyche, because He loves us. For the non-believer, we evolved to acknowledge the same set of rules out of our survival instinct. In either case, we pretty much all agree that the same set of rules apply for the game of life.

In a household, one of the things that Moms and Dads have to do is provide the rules. As long as the kids abide by the rules, they can live their lives with joy. When the rules get broken, well, there just ain't as much joy.

One of the biggest issues that we have in society today is that no one wants to play by the rules. We think that freedom is all about doing whatever we want. Well, that is just wrong headed. Freedom is not about doing whatever we want. It is doing what we want as long as it doesn't break the rules of society. Every law that is written has the limitations that your freedom cannot impede the freedom of another individual.

And oh by the way, just because an act is legal does not mean it is the right thing to do. When you perform an act that hurts another person, regardless of legality, it breaks the rules. You can't go around hurting other people. We seem to have this uncanny ability as humans to come up with new and creative ways to hurt each other. Then we say, "Well, there's no law against it." The next thing you know we have to pay Congress to write a new law, because some clown never learned the Ten Commandments from his Dad.

One other point on this, and it doesn't matter if you are Christian, Jew, Moslem, Hindu, Buddhist, Atheist or anything in between. If you know the basic rules of society, then you stand a pretty good chance of getting along. If you claim to be a Judeo-Christian, then you better know and follow all Ten. If you are not religious, just learn the last eight and pass them along to your kids. These rules are a good start to learning everything you need to know about living a life full of joy. And by the way, the Golden Rule (do unto others as you would have them do unto you) is a good summary of the Ten Commandments, and is accepted by pretty much every culture as well.

So with all due respect to my Christian Brothers and Sisters, and the countless men and women who have translated the Ten Commandments from Hebrew, to Greek, to Latin, to English, I have taken the liberty of translating the Ten Commandments yet again, but this time, into MANSPEAK.

1) I'm God; I made you, worship me and nothing else,

2) Give me one day a week to honor the fact that I made you,

3) Don't swear,

4) Honor your parents and those with authority over you,

5) Don't hurt or kill others,

6) Don't mess around sexually,

7) Don't lie,

8) Don't steal,

9) Don't lust for your neighbor's wife,

10) Don't lust for your neighbor's goods.

That's it, all Ten. They are called Commandments for a reason ... when we play by these rules, we all get along, and we are free to live in the joy that we desire.

When we break the rules, joy flies out the window, our lives turn to a mess and eventually society breaks down. It is a historical pattern. Egyptians, Persians, Greeks, French, Spanish, English ... every Empire since the dawn of history has fallen, because they didn't play by this set of rules. If you don't believe me ... ask the Romans. Case closed!

MAN UP Memos

- ✔ All Dads want to bring Joy to their children.
- ✔ Rules allow children to operate safely and joyfully.
- ✔ Children will not like the rules.
- ✔ The Ten Commandments are the basic rules of society.
- ✔ Learn the rules and model them for your children.

Love First, Rules Next

For each of my kids, there is one special mental picture that I can always return to. With my son, it was the day that we brought him home from the hospital. He was born about eight PM on a Sunday night. The hospital was of course ready to get us out as soon as they had counted all of the fingers and toes. We took him home the next day and by the time we got him home, both my wife and I were just wore out. I helped her get comfortable to take a nap, picked up my son, and laid him right in the middle of my chest. She napped, he napped, and I was the proudest Daddy that ever walked the face of the earth! This was a bonding experience that I will remember until the day I die.

The ability of a Dad to bond with his child is one of the greatest gifts of our generation. For centuries, all of the bonding happened between Mom and the child. Mom feeds, Mom bathes, Mom rocks, burps, changes — it was all about mother / child bonding. For a Dad, to be able to actively participate in the rearing and care of an infant is one of the true joys in life.

In my view, you really aren't a Dad until you've experienced the three P's. You have to be peed on, puked on and pooped on to be a Dad. If you haven't had all three ... repeatedly ... you are not close enough and frankly you probably aren't giving your wife enough help. The closer you are to your children in each phase of your child's life, the more they know that you love them.

Once you have built that bond, the child pays attention to you. Once he pays attention to you, he'll listen to you and you'll be able to influence the child and guide the child with love.

The love that you develop with a child needs to be continually reinforced. They need to hear that they are loved; they need to see that they are loved; they need to feel that they are loved. A child needs to be loved by both parents and a child needs to see that his parents love each other. A friend told me that he was a really good kid, until his parents separated. After that, he didn't feel it was necessary to pay attention to the rules because his parents didn't live up to the rules either. You know ... the one about "Till death do us part."

Children start out by emulating the environment within which they were raised. If it is a positive, loving environment, then the odds are they will try to repeat that. If it is a negative environment, they will have learned the bad and will not have a positive reference from which to grow. To turn out right, he will have to overcome the bad environment, a tough challenge for anyone, especially someone without a positive role model.

Another point on love, a child's psyche doesn't know, unless it is continually reinforced. Their minds are not mature enough to rationalize that they are loved the way that an adult can. My daughter tells us that every time my wife and I had a squabble, my daughter worried that we were about to get a divorce. Now, my wife and I had our spats but it never crossed our minds that we would ever divorce. Our fights were just run of the mill things that were never any jeopardy to our marriage. Unfortunately, our daughter did not share that understanding. She did not realize that two people could love each other and still have disagreements or squabbles. Her knowledge of love was still incomplete.

First and foremost, throughout a child's life, they need to feel love and see love acted out. If a child is loved and knows it, he will go out of his way to return that love. Humans are just built that way. But at some point, (like as soon as they can move) you are going to have to introduce rules (primarily for their safety). The reason for rules is to teach and protect the child. If a child knows that the reason for the rules is to protect him, he is a lot more likely to follow them.

When a child follows the rule, they need to be praised; when they break the rule, they need to suffer the consequence. Positive and negative reinforcement is how we learn. But a child always needs to know that they are still loved, even when being punished. If a child ever thinks that because they have broken the rules, they are no longer loved, you have just lost. Discipline alone won't cut it. The only reason for a child to want to follow the rules is to please a loving parent. Without love, a parent is nothing more than a rulebook attached to a vending machine.

Here is one last train of thought about love. Several years ago, my wife and I read a book, I will unabashedly plug. It was called *The Five Love Languages* by Gary Chapman. The pretext of the book is that humans by their nature share and receive love via one of five primary "love languages." Some people like gifts, others words of love, some crave time together, others need caring gestures, and some respond best to physical touch.

The book was written for couples to heighten the awareness of love language between spouses. Basically, if a husband wants to communicate that he loves his wife, he needs to figure out what her love language is and communicate his love to her in the language she understands. If he communicates in HIS language, he may be sending the signal, but she isn't receiving the message the way she needs to hear it. It is kind of like him speaking English, but her only understanding Spanish. He may think he's communicating his love, but she just may not comprehend.

The reason for going through this explanation is simple. Kids are people too. If you really want to let a kid know that you love them, figure out their love language and talk to them in THEIR language. Some kids crave time, others kind words, some need gifts, others need lots of hugs. The point is ... find out what your kids need to let them know you love them, and pull a Nike ... just do it!

MANUP Memos

- ✔ Love builds bonds with your children.
- ✔ Make sure your kids know they are loved.
- ✔ People have different Love Languages.
- ✔ Learn the language that matches your spouse and kids.

Dad's Job

I mentioned in the introduction to this book that I have spent the better part of my life in corporate America, building what most would view as a very successful career. It was pretty typical for me to leave at seven in the morning and get home between seven and eight at night, for well over 25 years. During that time, I received lots of promotions, completed a degree, moved to three states for work and several other times for bigger and nicer homes.

Before we married, my wife and I compared notes on how we wanted to raise our children. We were both raised in an environment of a working Dad and a stay-at-home Mom. We thought it had worked out well for us and we decided that we wanted to raise our children in the same manner. We made a conscious decision that economics would take a second seat to our family and that as a result, we would defer the "cool toys" and big vacations, so that one of us would be there when the kids left for school and when they got home.

I am convinced that, in the long run, this is best overall for the kids and it would keep a whole lot of kids out of Juvenile Hall if more parents did the same. You won't recognize the impact that this approach makes on a kid's life until your children are raised and one day they come up to you and thank you just for being there.

My wife is especially grateful that she was always available to listen to our children when they most needed it. Sometimes it was on the way home from school, or during snack time after they got home. Sometimes it was just before bed. You never know when a child needs you the most. But part of your job is for you or Mom to be there to listen. Not only will it have an impact on them, it will go a long way to build the relationships that you will need as they approach puberty.

Now don't sit back and say, "Well, we can't afford that." Now I'm going to play the BS card. You can ... it is just the choices that you choose to make. What are you going to prioritize, the new car, the big screen TV or your kids? It is that simple. You figure out what is more important.

Anyway, while my career was going on, we had three kids. They were involved in kid stuff: soccer, basketball, dance team, karate, kickball, church groups, etc. and, fortunately for us, my wife was always there to do most of the "heavy lifting" when it came to carting them around. She was also the one there to put up with all of the kid "stuff"; the attitudes, the squabbling, the bickering, the wounds, crises and successes; all of the things that happen in the normal day to day process of growing up.

As we all know, time doesn't stop, and unlike a video game, you don't get a redo. I have lost that time and I will never get to see my child's first goal or dance routine or song recital. Looking back with hindsight, I realize a few things that I would redo if I could.

First, I spent way too much time working and not near enough time with my wife and kids.

Second, the minute that I left the last job, I realized all the time I spent there and not with my family seemed like a waste. Frankly, the company doesn't care who you are or what you contribute. The only ones that really care are your wife and kids. **Make sure you put your family first.**

Third, my wife and I have completely different parenting styles that, in my view, are pretty complementary. She always wanted to explain to the kids why things needed to be a certain way. I would listen to her trying to explain, the kids pushing back, and squabbling back and forth with their Mom. I would listen just long enough to get to the point of "It's my way or the highway." I guess maybe I should have explained a little more and, maybe with a little less explanation on her part, there wouldn't have been as much frustration.

All in all though, I think we have been a pretty good team! I guess the point of this whole chapter is: Guys, LIFE IS SHORT. You need to work enough to get the job done, but not so much that you take too much time away from the family. If the job demands too much, then it isn't the right fit for you. Your family comes first. On the day you walk out of work, the company will replace you and keep on rolling. With your family, on the day you walk out, it will never be a family again. You can be replaced at work. You can't be replaced in your family.

Pay attention here because this is very important. YOUR FIRST AND MOST IMPORTANT JOB IS TO BE A HUSBAND AND DAD!

MANUP Memos

- ✔ Your most important Job is to be a Dad.
- ✔ Moms and Dads have different, complementary parenting styles.
- ✔ A company can always replace you.
- ✔ A family can never replace you.

Boys and Girls

Last week my wife and I were sitting in church and saw a young couple with kids sitting in front of us. The Daddy was holding a five year-old girl. The older brother, nine or so, was sitting next to them and the Mom was next to the boy.

The little girl was clearly relishing her position, hugging and kissing her daddy throughout the service, occasionally glancing down at her brother. The Dad was stroking her hair and hugging back. The little boy just watched, and occasionally would reach over and softly touch his Dad's arm. Not to gain his attention, but to just reach out to him. And true to form ... Dad never acknowledged the boy was even there.

The Mommy was watching what was going on and quietly teared up. My wife sat there, also with tears in her eyes, watching the Dad fawn over the little girl, while ignoring the boy all together. After the service, she went up to the young man, smiled, shook his hand and quietly whispered in his ear, "Your son needs you too!"

This sort of thing happens all the time. Some men are really uncomfortable showing affection to their sons, others have a problem showing affection to their daughters. Daddy's listen up; it doesn't matter if they are boys or girls, the kids need you and they need you to show them that you love them.

The nice thing is that until children start reaching puberty, there really isn't a lot of difference between the two. Oh, the activities or the interests may be a little different, but hugs and kisses are just hugs and kisses. Time spent together with Daddy is special, no matter the sex of the kid. And believe me, Mom will appreciate the break that she gets any time you are taking the kids off her hands!

Of course, once they become teenagers, it is quite natural for you to completely lose your ability to communicate with your daughter. C'mon guys, you know what a boy is going through and what he is thinking, but once a little girl starts turning into a woman ... well ... how well do you really understand a grown up woman? Much less one that is just trying to figure it out!

The more time you spend building relationships with your kids before they turn into teenagers, the better off you will be on keeping some degree of sanity while they are teenagers. And as teenagers it is absolutely critical that you have the sort of communication where you can talk and coach them through everything from asking for a first date to breaking up with the "love of their life."

It is the teenage years that determine the kind of Dad that you have been. Once they become teenagers, it is too late for you to demonstrate a bunch of "newfound skills." You had your chance to form them when they were young, malleable and impressionable. As teenagers, your ability to guide them shrinks as they spend less time at home and more time with their "heathen" friends. The influence from their friends becomes a huge amount of pressure. And as they age, the only thing that will keep them out of trouble is the coaching they have received in the past and their willingness to talk to you and Mom.

So Dads, **take care to love your sons and daughters**. Make sure they both have a special place in your heart, and if you aren't sure how to love your son ... ask yourself how you wish your father had behaved towards you. If you aren't sure how to love your daughter, ask your wife how she wished her Dad had loved her.

MANUP Memos

- ✔ Show affection to your sons and daughters.
- ✔ Build the relationships with the kids when they are young.
- ✔ Keep the relationships with the kids as they age.

Parent's Roles

One of the cool things about writing a book like this is that sometimes I get to point out the obvious that never dawns on most people. That makes these next two chapters a lot of fun.

In every relationship, each player has a role. The roles are different, but the roles define a lot about how the relationship will play out. In a family, there are parent's roles and kid's roles. And the roles are different. When families appropriately demonstrate those roles, things go along pretty well. When families don't demonstrate those roles, things pretty much go down the tubes.

I am not going to get into the differences of the roles of Mom versus Dad, but believe me those roles are different. It is very important to have both a Mom and a Dad because they balance each other out. But, here we are going to talk about the parental role as a singular. The reason for this is pretty simple. Parents are not dealing with rational, adult minded people. It takes a coordinated effort on the part of both parents to raise a child without losing your mind (at least temporarily).

Parents think, often wrongly, that kids can be reasoned with, are logical and are just little adults that can be trusted. Guys this is fallacy. Kids aren't adults. They don't think the same way as adults, their brains are not physically complete, their hormones are not fully under control, their only predictability comes from recognizing that you were once a kid, and that they will most likely repeat all of the stupid things that you once did.

Children can only be trusted to the point that their brains and learning have progressed. If you give them too much latitude you will be scratching your head wondering what went wrong. If you don't believe me, just ask God.

He is the perfect parent. He gave us a pretty logical set of rules but we have gone absolutely crazy trying to get around every rule we have been given. So, if by nature, humans try to break the rules, then why on earth would you think that your kids are any different? They are from you!

Now that I've put things into perspective, there are a few pointers that I would like to share. First, if you are wise enough to know the role of the parents and the role of kids, things can be a little easier. Second, kids at an early age are trainable. If you train them to play by the rules when they are young, the odds are they will continue to follow the rules as they age ... to a certain extent. Third, and this is important, if you cannot control a kid when he is two, you don't stand a snowball's chance in hell of getting him under control when he is fifteen. Parenting isn't a sprint. It's a marathon. You have to use the same skills for 18 to 22 years. You'd better learn to parent early or your life will be miserable.

Now here is the good stuff. Remember when we talked about the Ten Commandments? Well, that is the pattern; all we have to do is follow it. A parent's role is pretty simple:

- Love always.

- Provide rules that help your children learn, keep them safe, and prevent them from harming others.

- Make sure they are rewarded for positive behavior and punished for negative behavior.

If you do these things consistently, I promise that you have done all you can to raise your kids the right way. In all likelihood, you will be blessed with good kids!

When you look at that problem kid in the grocery store, one of a few things will stand out: he clearly doesn't know how to conduct himself, (he doesn't know the rules), or the parent threatens but never disciplines (no or inconsistent consequences for bad behavior). Odds are that if the kid is out of control in public, he is a total brat at home. In spite of lots of yelling or spanking the parents have no clue how to control him. They are just waiting to get him out of the house. Whew!

Folks, there just aren't that many children that need to be on medication. Most of them just need a parent that knows his role and knows how to deliver. Watch "Super Nanny" on TV. She goes into a home that is a wreck, sets some rules, delivers some consequences and within a week, walks out having provided a turnaround for a family that a week before was ready to kill each other. This isn't a miracle. She is teaching the parents their role and the kids theirs as well.

Here is the secret: **A parent's role is to set the rules and enforce them consistently. A kid's role is to continuously push the rules.** That's their job. That's how they grow and learn how to survive, by pushing the envelope. It isn't any different than the settlers moving west. They didn't like the rules of the crowded east, so they changed the rules. That is all that kids are doing.

The biggest difference between a kid pushing the rules and an adult is this: the kids don't have the knowledge and wisdom to know what is safe and what isn't. Their brains haven't developed that filter yet. Because they haven't developed the "It's Not Safe" filter, it is the parent's job to make sure that the rules are appropriate, and followed. When a child starts breaking the rules, they are jeopardizing their own happiness or health or someone else's. That is why the parent has to set the rules and make sure they are enforced properly.

Here's another bit of wisdom: **If you set rules that you aren't going to enforce, you are just teaching your child that no rule is important.** You are reinforcing the behavior that he can break the rule and get away with it. Folks, this is where criminals come from. They learn at home that they can break the rules and get away with it.

Now that we are talking about rules, let's get another thing or two out. First, we have established that the parent has to set the rules. Make sure that the rules are appropriate for the development and maturity level of the child. As he grows and shows some responsibility, lighten up on the rules. You don't want a toddler running around the block, but by the time a child is eight or nine, he should be sharp enough to navigate his way home. Also, make sure that the rules are appropriate for the surroundings. The rules are there to keep a kid safe. Just because a child can walk around the block in suburbia, that doesn't mean you would let him do the same thing if you were living in a neighborhood surrounded by street gangs.

Second, it is ok to negotiate with the kids a little but once the deal is set, stick to your guns. If you and the child negotiate to a curfew, then you have to hold them accountable to live to the curfew. If you don't, he just learned that you are a pushover.

Finally, you need to live up to your side of the bargain. If you set the rules and the child lives by them, and you still aren't happy with the results then tighten the rules the next time. Don't punish him for playing by the rules.

When I was a boy, I hung out a lot with my Dad. As a result, he had a pretty good idea of my level of responsibility. He knew that I had a job, had paid for my own car, was always at work on time, and kept my grades up. As a result, I never had a curfew, because he could see that I was a self-starter.

My senior year, I was going to a party across town, and my Mom, who was always a worrier, told me to wake her up when I got home. To make a long story short, I was driven home by my friend's Dad, got home way too late, and was clearly under the influence. But I did make it down the hall and wake up my Mom.

My Mom was AS MAD AS A HORNET! The next morning, I woke up and felt like death warmed over but still had to go to work. I heard my folks arguing about what to do about my behavior. Then I heard my Dad, (the real hard case) tell her, "Don't say a word about it; he did exactly as you told him."

I learned a lot from that episode. First, I realized that I had broken an unspoken rule and violated their trust, something I never did again. I also learned that while I had screwed up, they were willing to cut me a little slack, because I had followed the rules and suffered the consequences.

As a parent, you want your children to know that the rules are there for their safety and to help them grow up. Don't burden the child with a lot of unnecessary stuff, but make sure the rules teach them how to contribute as an adult and grow up safely.

The last thing I want to discuss about parent's roles is that there are always two parents! (Remember biology!) You guys have to work together. Mom can't have one set of rules and Dad the other. If you do this, the kids will just divide and conquer. (Remember this phrase, it will help you when your kid uses this tactic.) Never debate the rules in front of your children. Ever. They will see this as a sign of weakness. If you and your spouse are not 100% aligned, then table the discussion, go behind closed doors and work it out privately so when you return with a unified front, the kids know there isn't any wiggle room.

My wife and I have done this consistently for years and it works like a champ. Our children know that she is the easier one to move, and they know that I am typically the hard case. But when they hear the same story from the both of us, they know that their mother is conveying the message, but that I have her back, and if they keep pushing the envelope, I will settle it.

Using this approach, my wife and I can make sure the rules are age and situation appropriate, applied fairly and will be consistently enforced. Our kids can see the unified front, and they know that the boundaries are clear, well defined and that we agree as parents that this is best for their growth and their safety.

Finally, as parents, there are times when you just have to put your foot down. This is your job and the safety or future of your child may depend on it. You and your wife both have this responsibility, but if the two of you can't get aligned then, Dad, it falls on you. Somebody has to be the leader and frankly, Dad, when push comes to shove, that's you.

Once on a business trip, as I stepped on an elevator, a mom, dad and teenage daughter got on as well. They were a normal looking couple in their mid 40's, middle class, nothing spectacular. The daughter, on the other hand, had a face full of tattoos and metal studs projecting from her lips, nose, eyebrows and pretty much everywhere else.

I wanted to take the Daddy out and whip his butt! This clod had either allowed his daughter (or his wife and daughter) to permanently mar her face in a manner that she will be dealing with for the rest of her life. By caving in to a fad, he allowed his daughter to do something permanent that can't be changed. Clothes and hair can change. But permanent modifications to the body, made by a sixteen year old "decision maker" ... that just tells me that they have bigger problems than they know how to deal with.

Guy's, you were all young, once. You know where the landmines are, the decisions that are temporary and the ones that are permanent. It is your job to not allow your kid to make a decision that will negatively affect their lives, their livelihood, and their future. MAN UP.

MAN UP Memos

- ✔ Rules are intended to keep children safe and allow them to grow.
- ✔ Children do not know what is safe and what isn't.
- ✔ A parent's job is to set the rules.
- ✔ A parent's job is to enforce the rules consistently.

Kid's Roles

In the previous chapter I already alluded to the role of kids. Their job, by nature, is to find the boundary conditions, to push the edge and to stretch themselves physically and mentally. That is how we, as humans, grow. And that is how, as kids, they try to drive parents crazy!

I will admit to this; they aren't trying to drive us crazy on purpose. It is mostly by accident and, generally, it is our fault. The reason it bothers us so much is that we haven't realized that it is their job! We think that they are like us--rational, logical and aware of the surroundings. We have totally forgotten that we were once like them. We drove our own parents nuts. We pushed the edge. We did stupid stuff. We were the ones getting grounded or bragging when we thought we were getting away with it!

It took us years to get to the point where we realized that **there is a cause and effect between decisions that we make and the progress that we see in our lives**. Our children just haven't gotten there yet. So yes, by nature, their job is to break the rules either intentionally or accidentally.

Once, when I was a teenager, I quite logically and rationally reasoned that someone needed to go feed our horse. Dad was out of town and Mom had left the house early. So, in my mind, the responsibility had fallen to ... ME. Although I had never driven a standard shift car, I had watched my Dad do it a thousand times. So I logically reasoned that I could hop in the Jeep, drive to the horse lot, feed the horse, and that I, ultimately, would have done my parents a big favor! I wasn't intentionally being bad. I had reasoned through the decision, logically weighed the options, and decided that I would teach myself how to drive before sunup. And by doing this, I was actually performing a much-needed service, for which my parents would be grateful.

This is just an example of how "kid logic" works. I had endangered myself and others, had jeopardized my Dad's Jeep and had jeopardized my recently earned driver's license. This was all because I did not fully recognize the risks or my own limitations.

By the time the episode was over, I had learned how to drive the Jeep, had gotten back home and in the garage without an accident and my parents didn't find out about it until I told them, like 20 years later. So it all worked out. I had stretched my boundaries and gotten away with it. I also knew that if my parents had found out, I probably wouldn't have driven a car until I graduated from college!

Now, how many kids do you think have "appropriated" Mom and Dad's car? My guess is probably greater than 50%. At least one of my kids did it. (She got caught by scraping the side view mirror on the garage on the way back in.) The fact is you and I know that when we were kids, we bent or broke the rules. All kids do.

This is one of the tools that we can use, as parents, to keep our kids safe. Don't stick your head in the sand. Don't think your kids are devils OR angels. Recognize them for what they are, just kids. Recognize that their job in life is to grow and learn and that your role is to allow them to do this with sufficiently safe and appropriate boundaries. The boundaries are there so they can make it to adulthood all in one piece.

There is no need to be at war with your kids. When the tensions are high it may be hormones, it may be your rules are too strict, it may be something is seriously bad in their life or it may be that they just need some space to grow. Learn to find out what is going on and help guide them through it. But remember: **you set the rules, you enforce the rules**. It is your job to determine if the rules are appropriate and fair, not theirs. You have the wisdom and the practical experience to make the determination, not them. Although it is nice if you can be your kid's best friend, you have to make a choice. There are hundreds of people that can be your kid's best friend, but only you can be their dad. Only you are responsible for your kid's well being and safety.

They will want rules that give themselves unconstrained freedom to operate without regards to risk or their own limited capabilities. Your job is to make sure that the rules protect them while balancing their need to grow and experience new frontiers. Use the knowledge and wisdom that your experience has given you. You have the wisdom to strike a balance. Use that wisdom and authority to give your kids the chance to grow safely and securely!

MANUP Memos

- ✔ Kids do not follow adult logic.
- ✔ A kid's job is to break the rules.
- ✔ They are programmed that way; it's how they learn.
- ✔ Your rules are there to protect them from their own bad decisions.
- ✔ Kids won't like the rules, but they will get over it.

Discipline: Yours and Theirs

One thing about all discipline is that it is painful. It is painful for you as a parent; it is painful for the child. No one ever likes to give or receive discipline. It is unpleasant.

Discipline is also a part of life. A child that is raised without discipline is not prepared for the future. Life is not all about the child getting what he wants, doing what he wants and acting the way he wants. He will learn discipline one way or the other. It is much better that a child learns discipline from someone who loves him and who will make it appropriate, than for his first taste of discipline to be from the guy who pounds him into a mud hole because your kid did something that was out of line.

Your child will be disciplined at some point. If you are a Dad, you would rather do it yourself than have it done for you.

If you look around, the world is full of undisciplined children. The schools are full of children who disregard parents, teachers and pretty much everyone. This in my view is 100% the parents fault. **Any parent who doesn't teach their child the word "NO" ... and mean it ... is doing the child a disservice.**

If you look at the chapter title, though, this chapter is about your discipline and theirs. So let's break it down.

First, you have to be disciplined in your own conduct. The child is going to learn how to conduct himself by watching you. How do you treat others (especially mom and the siblings)? What type of language do you use? Do you conduct yourself with dignity? Do you over indulge with food, drink, etc? Are you rude? These are all of the traits that a child will pick up on just by watching your behavior. You are a role model and if you aren't pleased with the behavior of your child, then look at your own behavior first. And oh, by the way, remember those Ten Commandments. They are a good measuring stick for yourself and for your kids. Learn them and use them to measure your own discipline first. Then, you can reasonably expect your kids to live up to the same expectation.

Ok, so now that you are doing your best to lead a disciplined life, let's talk about your approach to discipline. You need to have a systematic approach. For discipline to be effective, it needs to be appropriate for the situation, for the age of the child and for the severity of the offense. Discipline needs to be consistently applied and it needs to be something that works for that particular child.

Using the same disciplinary approach, in all instances, doesn't work. He or she will get accustomed to it and then the discipline no longer serves as effectively. You have to be the judge as to the effectiveness and periodically change your game. If it gets to the point that discipline no longer serves as a deterrent for behavioral change, it isn't effective any longer and you have to make some modifications.

Let's talk about that word "deterrent." As I mentioned earlier, people learn behavior by positive reinforcement for good behavior and negative reinforcement for bad behavior. If a child learns about positive and negative reinforcement at an early age, then the anticipation of positive or negative reinforcement is enough to guide the behavior.

In other words, the more you love them, the more that they associate love with good behavior, the more that they will strive to demonstrate good behavior. But when they exhibit bad behavior and they receive prompt negative reinforcement, they quickly correlate the two and they learn to avoid bad behavior in order to avoid the negative repercussions. Knowing that the discipline will occur serves as a deterrent to prevent bad behavior.

This is where a lot of parents blow it. When they see bad behavior, they scold, they threaten, they warn. But, nothing ever happens. The child knows that the parent's threats are all smoke and that nothing ever occurs to correct their behavior. They learn that the parents are bluffing without any follow up. Just like in Poker, the kids will place the bet and WIN!

A child needs to know exactly where the boundary is and that you will let the hammer down as soon as they cross the boundary. If they know the rules, and they know the repercussions, they are making the choice to comply or not and they learn to suffer the consequences. If parents are consistent and the child knows the rules, the parents don't go crazy and the child learns to live by the decisions that they make.

You particularly see this pattern when you have two parents: one that tries to talk to them without end and the other that just draws the line. Some kids act like heathens around one parent and will fly the straight and narrow around the other. They are just responding to the inconsistency in parenting styles. As I said, a kid's job is to push the boundaries. They know the soft borders with one parent and the hard borders with the other and adjust accordingly.

You and your spouse have to get aligned for discipline to work. You have to agree on how the boundaries will be set, and what the various levels of discipline will be. This is for the parents to decide. If you and your wife come to agreement while heads are cool, then when the time comes to drop the hammer, it is just a matter of execution.

Now I want to shift gears a little and talk about discipline from the kid's perspective. The first thing is that no one disciplinary approach works for all kids. Just as people have love languages, they also have things that really bother them. If you can figure out the love language that energizes your child and the disciplinary approach that affects them the most, you have two very powerful tools.

Here are a couple of examples: I knew a guy in high school that had an extremely high tolerance for pain. For someone like him, corporal punishment would never work. It didn't bother him at all. His parents would have to come up with something that affected him for the discipline to work.

For another example, my daughter was always a very social person. She wanted to be the center of attention and around people all of the time. My wife and I figured out that when she misbehaved, the worst possible punishment for her was to be sent to her room ... ALONE. Five minutes alone in her room would straighten her right up.

The trick is to find the punishment that fits the child. No two kids are alike so just pay attention to their personality and find the discipline that fits.

Another thought: **don't wear it out or rule it out**. Using the same discipline over and over just allows the kids to anticipate and build up a tolerance. And, if you rule something out (like corporal punishment) you may be taking the one tool off the table that will work for that particular child. Never rule things out. Having control over the finances, car keys and even the college purse strings are all tools that the parent needs to have at their disposal while you are guiding the child.

Another point about discipline: **don't discount the effectiveness of a good BLUFF**. In most cases, all it takes is for the child to think that you will follow up on the discipline. A knowing glare from Mom or Dad can be very effective in keeping your kid in check.

Always remember that if you lose control of a child at two or three you will never get it back when he is a teenager. Every teacher (or Drill Instructor) knows that it is better to start out tough and lighten up as things go on.

Finally, and this is very important: **Make sure that the child always knows that you still love them.** If they are choosing to behave poorly, then they are choosing to receive the discipline. You never want the child to think that you don't love them and you certainly don't want them to think that you are enjoying disciplining them.

They need to learn that there are good and bad actions and good and bad consequences to those actions. Properly applied discipline is an opportunity to teach them a life lesson (as well as to keep them from disturbing you, the rest of the neighborhood, and possibly avoiding some really bad consequences).

MAN UP Memos

- ✔ No one likes discipline.
- ✔ Your kid will be disciplined from you or from life — it's better from you.
- ✔ You must show self-discipline to expect discipline from them.
- ✔ You must be consistent in discipline.
- ✔ Don't wear it out or rule it out.
- ✔ Use appropriate discipline for the child and situation.

YOUR RESPONSIBILITY IN GROWING UP

As parents, you've been there. You have lived through childhood, the teen years and the growing pains of young adulthood. You have had your share of good and bad experiences, of good and bad parenting, of accidents and mishaps, of successes and cherished memories.

Your job as a parent is to help your child navigate those same experiences: sharing the joys, encouraging them when they start a new adventure and providing a safety net for their earliest attempts at adulthood.

Your job is to share your history, coaching them, not doing it for them, warning them of the risks and dangers and allowing them to try, to succeed or to fail. They have to have all of those experiences. Yours isn't to live the experiences for them or to protect them from failure. Your job is to help them to grow through all of those things and only protect them when catastrophic failure is a high probability.

Life is a combination of good and bad. They have to be able to experience both. You can't live for your child. And you have to allow them to win or lose on their own. This is the only way that they will be able to correlate their efforts and the rewards that life will give them. They also have to experience the failures. Without a little rain, they won't appreciate the sunshine.

But as I mentioned earlier, a kid doesn't know the difference between a short-term risk and a decision that will affect his life forever. You cannot delegate a decision to a child that has adult ramifications. Your job is to prepare them to be mature enough to make a good decision when the time for adult decisions come upon them.

My own parents did a great job of this. At an early age Dad taught us to work and to give it our best when we did work. He taught us to save a portion of our earnings and he taught us how to bank and pay the bills. He taught us to act like adults when we were around adults and he taught us to show respect for our elders.

My Mom taught us how to love and how to care for another person, how to laugh and enjoy life. My Mom taught us how and when to communicate, how to snuggle a kid, how to be affectionate and to show a child that they were always loved.

These were life lessons that my folks taught us by demonstration. They lived their lives as good and decent people and we watched them and we learned from them. Were they perfect? Heck no! We learned from their mistakes, as well. There were lots of things that my parents did that I have chosen not to do. But as everything else in growing up, **you take the good and build on it, and you take the bad and avoid it.** This is what you are trying to show your children.

And just to put it a little in perspective, all you are trying to accomplish is to do a little better job for your kids than your parents did for you. It's all about evolution. If you can make the next generation just a little better, then you have done your job.

MANUP Memos

- ✔ Your role is to guide your children.
- ✔ Don't live their lives for them.
- ✔ Use your own experience and wisdom to help them.

TIME WITH YOUR KIDS

In most kid's life, there are those special "Dad memories" that never wane. For me, it was when he and I had gone on a hunting trip to Colorado. We had gone up a day before the rest of our group to stake out camp. The first night we were up there, it was just the two of us. There probably wasn't another human for ten miles or so. Camped out at nine thousand feet, the stars looked like you could reach out and touch them.

This was one of those chances as a boy to really be alone, one on one, with my Dad. This is a memory that I will relish forever. But as meaningful as that memory was for me, it touched my Dad as well. Any time that he reflected on my years growing up, he would tell that story, only from his perspective. My Dad told that story for the rest of his life. This was one of those very rare instances where a father and son shared something that moved each of them, at the same time.

The key to having times like this is to spend time your kids.

With all of the hustle and bustle of the world, we often think that doing things in the same proximity is the same as spending time. Well, let me tell you, they are not the same. For you to really spend time with your child, at any age, you have to get to the point where you can focus on what is happening around you. Whether it is sitting alone together on a Daddy/Daughter date or spending a few hours together quietly fishing, you have to be together and alone for the magic to occur.

One of the little things that my daughters loved and recall, even now, is dancing with Daddy. I used to watch my Dad, with my sisters. They would put their feet on his and they would dance together in the living room. I never knew how powerful of a moment that was until I shared the same experience with my own daughters. To them, it was just the thrill of Daddy being totally focused on his little girl, even if it was just for a few minutes.

You really learn about your children, what makes them tick, and the kind of people they will be in moments such as these. My youngest daughter was always the precocious one; gregarious and outgoing, she was into everything, would try anything until she knew she could "do it" and then was ready to move on. My wife and I were always concerned about whether or not she would find her niche.

When it was time to have our family pet put down, she insisted that she would go with me. I watched my brave, little girl cradle our beloved Duchess into her arms just as she had as a puppy. She hugged her tightly as the needle was inserted and loved her as Duchess gently went to sleep. I realized, right then, just the kind of person that my little girl would grow to become and that I never had to worry about her.

These are the moments that come sporadically in life. As our society becomes more and more frantic, it is important for Dads to make sure that they make the time to be with their kids. Really BE WITH THEM. Spend family time together, share family meals, have quiet time with your kids, alone. It is through these times that they learn from you and you learn from them.

There is an old saying, "I've never seen an Epitaph that read; "I wish I had spent more time working." Brothers, this is a truism. As you get older, you will look back in time and realize how fleeting that time really is. You will realize how much you wish you had one more dance, or one more hunting trip, or listened to your child perform one more solo ....

When my Dad was lying in the hospital, shortly before his death, I was working several hundred miles away. I was driving every other weekend to come over and spend time with him, and to relieve my Mom at his bedside. By that time, Dad was pretty weak and really couldn't even say much. I would stand at the foot of his bed and massage his feet. I could see the strain lift from his face and the relaxation set in. I could picture the time that we spent together in Colorado ...

This is another father-son moment that I will cherish for the rest of my life. Quality time ... together ... alone ... quiet. Don't take the time that you have with your family for granted. God only gives each of us so much time; so make sure that you use that time with your kids wisely.

MANUP Memos

- ✔ Spend quality, quiet time with each child.
- ✔ Time with your family is more important than time at work.
- ✔ Don't take family time for granted; you will regret losing it.

COMMUNICATION

This is one area where I feel that my wife and I have done an outstanding job and an area where many parents fail miserably. You need to be able to speak to your child about any topic and, what is even more important; they need to be able to speak to you about any topic. There is no room for bashfulness because there are so many things out there today that can destroy a life. You have to be able to frankly discuss virtually any topic under the sun.

Now just to set things straight: there are family topics that a child has no business knowing, (like personal things that should be held in private between a husband and wife). Just because a child is curious, that doesn't mean that you have to answer every question.

However, there are topical matters that you should always be able to discuss with your kids: like sex, drugs, alcohol, pedophilia, birth control and abortion. Your children are exposed to these things every day. These things are happening in the schools, to your kid's friends and possibly to your own kids.

You have to be able to discuss these topics without shame and without blame. The number of children who are VICTIMS, that do not believe they could talk to their parents, is staggering. Most kids are ashamed to speak openly even when the topic is not their fault. I recently read a story of a young woman, who had two abortions after she went away to college. She never confided to her parents because they were staunchly pro-life and she didn't want to disappoint them. This sort of thing happens all the time.

Another thing to point out is that if you see a major behavioral change in your child, something has probably happened. Go find out what it is. A kid's personality doesn't just change overnight. You know your child, and it is your job to counsel and protect him/her.

If you see a new behavior that you can't explain: take a breath, have a seat and talk to them. And remember: this is about showing them love and that you care. You have to be just as willing to listen, as you are to speak.

My wife and I have been blessed with the ability to talk with our kids freely about anything. Our children know that any topic is open. We, as parents, have to be careful not to butt in and allow the child to have an ear when they need it. Develop the pattern of open communication at a young age. Early crises have a tendency to be easier to resolve. By beginning to communicate early, you will be ready when the big things start happening in the teens and early twenties. If your child knows they can depend on you when they are little, it will be easy for them to come to you as they get older.

And finally: when your child does come forward, it is ok to create a new rule to stop some destructive behavior or to avoid a bad situation. Sometimes, your child is looking for an out to avoid peer pressure. It can be a lot easier for a child to tell a friend, "My stupid parents won't let me," than it is to say, "I really don't want to do that."

MAN UP Memos

- ✔ Learn to communicate with your children.
- ✔ Communication means speaking with and listening to them.
- ✔ Communicate about anything and everything.
- ✔ Build communication when they are little or you won't have it when they are older.

RESPECT

If you look at the Ten Commandments, you can boil them all down to one of two words: Respect or Love. Respect is following a course of action, out of honor for the position that someone holds. Love is doing the right thing, because you have a deep regard for someone and you know that, by doing it, the other person will be pleased.

Your child will not love everyone that they come in contact with, for a variety of reasons. Teaching someone to love everyone and treat them properly out of love is a lifelong endeavor that is well beyond the scope of this book. Respect, however, can be taught and expected from a very young age and has no bearing as to the emotional attachment that your child may have to a person. Respect is about treating someone properly because they have a right to receive the honor or dignity as an individual.

Many children today have no clue how to render respect to their elders, those in authority or even their parents. This is a failure on the part of the parents to teach their children that every person is due respect as an individual. If more children had this attitude, many of the ills of our society would already be resolved.

When I was a child, we were taught to say "Yes Sir, No Sir," "Yes Ma'am, No Ma'am," and this was out of respect for our elders. We were taught to dress properly for an event and especially for going to church. We were taught that teachers, coaches, police, adults and especially our parent's friends were to be treated with a level of dignity that went beyond that of our own peers.

Something is missing in our society when a 65 year-old man goes to church in shorts and a T-shirt or walks out of the service before the pastor does. This is what we are teaching our children: that you don't have to respect an office, a position or even God.

Just watch what happens during a sports event. When a coach sees a bad call, he yells and screams at the ref. C'mon guys, I watched Tom Landry for 20 years and never saw him raise his voice to a side judge. In fact, when was the last time you saw an NFL coach wear a jacket and tie? You see, for Landry, coaching was his profession and he treated it as his profession — with a professional demeanor.

Now I, for one, do appreciate that most businesses have a casual day and don't require business suits. But, you have to admit we have lost something when our best attire is a golf shirt or when you see people at a funeral in a Budweiser gimme cap.

When Dads start expecting their children to demonstrate respect at home, it rolls over into their social life. When I see a kid acting up in the grocery store, I just can't imagine the kind of terror that he must be at home.

Dads, it starts with you. You need to instill a level of respect in your children. They need to start by respecting you and their mother. Why would you allow your child to sass you or their Mom? That is just a sign of disrespect. As I mentioned earlier, their job is to push the boundaries. But, it is your job to set the boundaries and hold them to the standards that you set.

The minute that you permit the kids to disrespect you, their mother, their grandparents, their home, you have allowed them to learn to disrespect others. If they don't have to respect those that gave them life, and that are paying for their upbringing, then why on earth would they have to respect anyone else?

Our nation is founded on laws. **Individual rights only extend to the point that they do not impose on another's rights.** Teaching your children to give others their due respect enables them to function as an equal part of the greater society. Teaching them respect for another will quite possibly prevent them from making some serious errors in judgment and may prevent a butt kicking or jail term to boot!

MAN UP Memos

- ✔ Teach your children to respect.
- ✔ Respect begins at home.
- ✔ If they don't respect you or your wife they won't respect anyone else.

Your Kids in Public

News Flash ... It is not cute to see someone else's kid running up and down the aisles in Church during the middle of the sermon, rolling his Hot-Wheels around on the pews, or doing cartwheels as the bride is taking her solemn vows.

Nor is it appropriate for someone to allow a child to disturb dinner at a restaurant. It burns me up, when a family takes their brood into a nice restaurant and then allows the kids to run, jump, scream, cry and otherwise make the meal miserable for the rest of the diners. A few months ago, my wife and I were in a nice restaurant and watched as a patron recognized a semi-famous person, introduced himself to the celebrity and then allowed his kid to disrupt the entire restaurant, while the Dad continued to schmooze with the "big shot."

I would bet that each and every one of you have witnessed similar or worse behavior. My question is, "Where are the parents and what are they thinking?"

Dads, you and Mom have to realize that it is your responsibility to teach the child how to behave in public. I can recall, at four or five years of age that I was taught how to conduct myself in public places. If I got out of line, I would be quickly escorted out of sight and sound of everyone else so I could get some "control assistance." I was never permitted to disturb others and it was totally impermissible to throw a temper tantrum in the public view.

For the vast majority of children, this is simply a matter of parents setting and enforcing boundaries. If the child wants to go where "big people" are, then the child needs to act like a big person. If they can't behave properly, they need to stay home with the babysitter.

Several years ago, my wife and I were meeting for dinner with a couple and their *two* sets of twins. They had adopted twins from China and the other set were their biological children. As it turns out, due to scheduling (and a really funny twist of fate), this family went from Zero to Four in about four months! Yep, they went from childless couple to having two sets of twins that were roughly four months apart.

So, my wife and I were having dinner with this young couple and their four ... count'em ... four ... two year olds. And, to make a long story short, it was one of the most surprising and pleasant experiences of my life! This couple had learned that by setting expectations, having reasonable discipline and being consistent with the kids, these children were very capable of going to dinner with Mommy and Daddy. Furthermore, the parents were able to go to a nice restaurant and have an adult conversation. The children politely ate their meals and chatted when they were spoken to. We even got hugs at the end of the night!

If this couple were capable of raising four youngsters with this sort of control, then there is no reason why any other Dad and Mom cannot do the same thing. Unfortunately, the typical pattern is kids with worse behavior than cattle or we watch Mom and Dad allow little Johnny to have a spat of the 80 decibel "Why's" in the middle of Grand Uncle Fred's Eulogy!

Listen up people; good child behavior in public is a sure sign of proper parenting. Be a good enough Dad to control your youngster in public or keep them in the cry-room or leave them with the babysitter until they can behave. You won't believe the effect peer pressure can have on your seven year old when he has to stay in the nursery, or on your 14 year old when they are still under the watchful eyes of a baby sitter!

MAN UP Memos

- ✔ Teach your children to behave in public.

- ✔ Public behavior is a sign of good or bad parenting.

SCHOOLWORK

I am about to say something sacrilegious to millions of parents and tens of millions of kids. Schoolwork is more important than athletics! There ... I've said it. In spite of the millions spent on football stadiums in every little town in the US; in spite of the hundreds of millions spent on collegiate athletics; in spite of all of the beer commercials featuring world famous athletes; schoolwork is still more important than athletics or any other childhood activity.

Let me explain. If you run the numbers: out of a typical 5A high school there are about 2500 students, about 80 of which will play high school football. This is about 3% of the student body. Of the 80 that play, 22 will start, which means that the other 60 are essentially "tackling dummies." They are just not gifted to the same level as the starters, yet they show for practice, ditch their classes and exhaust themselves just for the opportunity to stand on the sidelines and watch their buddies play.

Of the 80 that suit up for a given high school team, a lucky one or two may get an opportunity to play college ball. With literally hundreds of colleges out there, it still means that less than one half of one percent of high school students will ever make it to play at college level. And of all of the student athletes that graduate each year, less than one tenth of one percent of them ever make pro-level. In spite of all of the practice and efforts given over roughly 12 years of work, less than a tenth of one percent ever gets any payback. Folks, those are lottery odds!

Now, of the same 2500 students, how many of them do you think will need to be able to read, write, perform basic math and hold an intelligent conversation? Every single one of them! Even criminals and burger flippers need to be able to function at a high school level!

So why do parents let their kids slide on schoolwork in order to play volleyball, football, baseball, soccer, golf, sing, and play in the band?! People, we have it totally "bass ackwards."

Schoolwork has to come first, because each and every adult (yes, even the athletes) needs to be able to function, pay bills, shop and send an email. (Forget sending them to college, I am just talking about the kids being able to achieve a basic level of living.) If you are not requiring your children to do well in school, you are doing them a disservice.

It is guaranteed that your kid would rather do anything than study. They will be looking for every excuse to dodge books (except of course, doing their chores or picking up their own mess.) You, however, have to set the expectations. **The significance of schoolwork must be one of the boundary conditions that are non-negotiable.**

My wife and I were fortunate enough that we were able to send our kids away to college. But, the expectation for performance did not end when they left for school. As long as we were footing the bill, we held them accountable. We set a rule: Mom and Dad pay for grades X and above; kid pays for grades Y and below.

Believe me, when your child has to fork over birthday money to reimburse the folks for a college class they bombed, it will make a difference.

Schoolwork is just another area where you have to teach your children to shoulder their responsibilities. And it can't start in high school. When your child first goes to school, you have to set the pattern: study before play, homework before extracurricular activities. If you wait till your child is in high school, or worse yet college, before they learn decent study habits, you will either A) spend a boatload more on tutors or B) waste a lot of money on college classes, only to find that your child is not capable of the work required.

One last thing, and this doesn't just apply to the mediocre students. A friend's son attended a high school that was noted for its scholastic programs. The young man made straight A's, was the valedictorian, and received a full ride to a noted engineering school. This brilliant guy promptly pulled the first D of his life during his first semester. The valedictorian quickly realized that he had skated through high school and suddenly, for the first time in his life, was seriously in over his head.

Remember the story about Raj? Well, every brilliant person in every underdeveloped nation on our planet is looking for a chance to come to the good old U.S. of A. because our kids are academic pushovers. Dads, you have to do something about it. You know the level of effort that it takes for a kid to learn a football playbook. It is your job to make sure they are spending more time on the playbooks that will last them for a lifetime.

MAN UP Memos

- ✔ Schoolwork is more important than sports.
- ✔ Children will avoid schoolwork at all costs.
- ✔ You have to teach good study habits at home; it's your role.

WORK ETHIC

One of the things that concern me the most about today's young people is their work ethic. Many kids have grown up expecting Mom and Dad to provide everything for them, allow them to do pretty much anything they want and with little or no effort of their own. Many parents feel it is necessary to buy their kids a car. If you feel it necessary to buy them a car, make sure they understand you still control the purse strings. You see parents who will buy their teen a car, and then listen to back talk from them. This is just totally out of line.

When I grew up, the rules were pretty much like this: Mom and Dad paid for the roof, the food, appropriate clothing and an education. If we wanted anything more than that, the answer was, "Get a job." Quite frankly, this has served my siblings and me pretty well. Each of us held odd jobs, babysitting, lawn care, paper routes and service jobs. Each of us bought our own cars, paid for our own dates, "special" clothes and material items that we just had to have. Through this approach, my folks taught us to work hard, to save our proceeds and to be wise in our purchases.

One of my Dad's favorite sayings was, "The only job in the world where you start at the top is when digging a ditch." This was his way of telling us that in any position and at any company, you are going to have to start at the bottom. And through hard work, talent, and diligence you are going to rise to the appropriate level. If a child makes it through high school and has no sense of what the world expects, he is in for a rude awakening. If he makes it through college and thinks that automatically there will be a job waiting for him on the other end, he is in for a shock.

My wife and I were always aligned in wanting our kids to be able to stand on their own two feet. We wanted them to know that by providing food and shelter, the opportunity for a proper education and by teaching them how to survive, we had fulfilled our financial obligation to them. Our job was to teach them how to survive, how to contribute and how to make adult decisions. But, once they were on their own, they had the responsibility to fend for themselves.

A friend of mine shared with me the number of times that he has had to bail his son out of a problem situation. The young man was intelligent, educated and good looking. He also had problems with drugs, the law, was bad with his finances and was 35 years old. I asked my friend how many times that he had forced his son to really live with the consequences of his bad decisions. The answer was ... never.

Parents can enable negative behavior by being overly protective of a child. Sometimes, a parent has to allow a child to suffer the consequences of a bad decision so that they will learn from their mistakes. I suspect that my friend had been covering his son's mistakes since he was an infant and this young man was continuing a dependency on his parents, well into adulthood.

Dads, **you can love your child and still allow them to suffer the consequences of their decisions**. If a child learns the difference between right and wrong, good and bad decisions at an early age, this is a gift that they will be able to depend upon throughout their lives. If a child only learns to come to Mom and Dad to make it all work out, they are not learning the rules that they will need to function in society. Furthermore, in most cases a child will live longer than their parents. How will a dependent adult cope if Mom and Dad aren't there to bail them out?

A child needs to learn to work and to fend for themselves. They need to learn how to support a family and to make good career and financial decisions. You must ensure that your parenting approach will teach your child how to survive in a world that is more demanding, more competitive and one in which Mom and Dad won't always be around to pick up the pieces.

MAN UP Memos

- ✔ Teach your kids work ethic at an early age.
- ✔ Kids have to learn to survive without your assistance.
- ✔ Don't always bail them out or they will be overly dependent.

ACTIVITIES

I may have tipped my hand a little bit when I highlighted that schoolwork is more important than all of that other stuff. Well, activities are part of that other stuff. The point about activities, though, is not that they are unimportant. Activities are very important. It's just that too often you see parents, kids or both running themselves ragged on activities. The fact is that our society is way too busy and that everyone needs a little down time — including kids.

If a child spends seven hours in school and another two or three per day doing homework, then how in the world are they supposed to participate in two, three or four after-school activities? The answer is they can't, so something slips. And what is it? Most likely, the schoolwork or the homework slips. Because we all know that children make time to do fun stuff, but they are always looking for excuses to get out of schoolwork.

Activities are there to provide a release and to teach kids to work together in teams. But reflecting on the last chapter, parents wearing out cars running their children all over creation doesn't make sense, unless he/she is a real college or pro-level prospect. Pretty frequently, you hear of the parent who is running their kid to karate, soccer, band, youth group, and the Friday night game, all in the same week. It gets even more hectic when there is more than one child and you add a whole additional set of activities in totally different directions.

Whatever happened to the family meal? After school soccer, T-Ball, basketball and football, that's what happened. It used to be that, on Sunday, the family went to church together. Now they go to soccer leagues in a different city. The point is that your children are not learning about family time together. They are learning to live a frantic lifestyle.

A parent needs to step in occasionally and allow the child to idle down. When I was young, I used to love to wander out in the fields and forest near my house. I had time to think, to chill out. I knew that we, as a family, would have dinner together pretty much every night. We learned togetherness. We actually talked about what was happening in our lives.

Activities can have a positive influence on your children, but keep them in perspective. Schoolwork and family time must have a higher priority than activity time. My wife and I wanted our kids to participate in some group activity as a learning experience, but we limited it so they could maintain balance in their lives.

As an adult, you know how hectic that life can be and how much stress is induced because of too much activity. Don't make the mistake of allowing (or forcing) your children to be "activity junkies" any earlier than they have to be.

MAN UP Memos

- ✔ Activities are good as long as they don't detract from school or family.
- ✔ Kids can be too active for their own good.
- ✔ Don't turn your kids into activity junkies.

SERVICE

One of the greatest things that you can introduce to your child is service to others. This was really a shortfall in my own upbringing, but it was something that my wife and I learned from our children. As I grew up, my Mom and Dad were busy with raising five of us and coping with the business of life. It was only after my folks retired that I learned my Mom had been involved in service to the community.

Fortunately for us, as our kids were growing up, they were involved in youth groups at church. Through that activity, they were exposed to and embraced the pleasures of helping those in need. They had the chance to visit underprivileged neighborhoods and do repair work on homes. They helped tutor and mentor other children and in college they became involved in service organizations within their universities.

Not only did they enjoy learning new skills but also were exposed to lifestyles with which they were unaccustomed. They learned that sometimes bad things happen to good people and they learned that there are good people living in neighborhoods where my kids may have been afraid to travel.

The greatest gift that our children received from these experiences was the joy of freely giving of themselves to another human being. This joy is beyond that of being paid for a job; it comes from doing something for someone else with no expectation of recompense.

The ability to give, for giving's sake, is a pleasure and a treasure that you can share with your kids. They will watch you and learn from you. If they see you contributing to society, they will likely do so as well. The joy that comes about by assisting someone that needs help is a feeling that they will remember. Hopefully, it will move them to continue to serve. Our society needs more people who care and who will step up to help the less fortunate.

The warmth of a human being, who is appreciative, is something that everyone should experience. By encouraging your children to serve others, not only will you help society but you will give them the gift of Joy that cannot be duplicated in any other way!

MAN UP Memos

- ✔ It is important for kids to learn service to others.
- ✔ Serving those in need will help your children understand life.
- ✔ Service to others can bring bountiful Joy.

HIGHER EDUCATION

In most cases, the first time a child gets to really operate without a net is when they leave high school and move away for work, college or the military. While you have been raising little Johnny or Johnetta and have put up with all sorts of erratic behavior for the last four to eighteen years, this is the first time they are really flying solo.

First, in spite of all the bravado and show of confidence, for the most part, they are still scared to death. They are going to find out pretty quickly that they don't know it all. And yes, believe it or not, they are going to be missing you, Mom and Mom's cooking within the first week of school.

When my wife and I went to orientation for our son at Texas A&M, they told us that after two weeks they could identify all of the freshmen boys on campus. It is about two weeks after school starts, that all of the crisp White and Maroon shirts were gone and replaced by seas of pink! (It is amazing at how few boys know to sort clothes by color and to use different wash temperatures!)

The first few years out of high school are really the final preparation phase for life. Just because the child moves away and can vote doesn't mean they are automatically capable of operating the heavy equipment of life. In all likelihood, they will struggle with academics at some point, either due to subject matter, size of class, poor study habits, late nights and late mornings or due to the introduction of wilder friends and adult beverages.

If your son/daughter is financially independent and away from home, then you may not have much "say so" in the matter, but you can still provide some wisdom. Don't harp, don't pester, but guide when appropriate. If, however, you are helping to foot the bill, then you still deserve to "get what you are paying for." There is nothing wrong with a parent setting certain performance expectations and some minimum acceptable social behaviors if you are footing the bill.

My wife and I were blessed to be able to fund our children's college education. But, as part of this, we required them to attain certain grades. If they didn't make the grade, we didn't pay for the class. We also established targets for how long they had to complete their course of study. We paid for four years. After that, it would come out of their pocket. We were not about to cover college on the six-year plan!

We also provided some financial incentives. One of our children negotiated a plan using dual credit courses and summer-school. She was able to finish college early, and as a result she was able to pocket a little extra dough. By accomplishing her four years in three and a half, we allowed her to pocket the savings she generated and it gave her a nice little nest egg.

Be creative in coming up with ideas that ensure your child gets something out of college other than four years of party time. At the time of this printing, four years of college costs roughly sixty grand at a public university. If you were spending that on a car, you would make sure to get what you were paying for. Make sure that if you are going to spend that on your child's education, you get what you pay for, as well.

On another note, colleges and universities offer a great deal of extracurricular activities today. I highly recommend that, while your son/daughter spends ample time studying, they should also look into positive social activities. These are good for networking, developing friends, giving back to society, and frankly, keeping them out of trouble. Some kids have part time jobs. That is a great way for them to learn to grow, burn some time, make some extra coin, or help defray some of their college expense.

As parents, you have to realize that colleges can also be cesspools that teem with undesirable behavior. Hopefully, by the time they move away, your children have an internal compass to keep them out of trouble. But, just recognize that at college your child is going to be exposed to every possible aberration: all of the things that you have tried to protect them from for the past 18 years.

One of the best things that you can do is to explain bluntly to them exactly the things to which they will be exposed. They will face decisions and risks to their life and livelihood that are serious, and of which they are probably ignorant. This is no time to pull punches. The more graphic you can be, the more likely they are to remember the elevator speech. And for gosh sakes, make sure that your teen knows that the best way to stay out of trouble is to avoid locations where trouble lurks.

College sponsored social programs ... Good thing: Freshmen going to un-chaperoned Toga Parties at Frat house ... Bad thing! By this time, it is too late just to tell a teenager what not to do and expect them to follow it.

But, the more that you explain *why* things are risky the more they will remember. Telling them *what* to do is training but it doesn't work at college age. Telling them *why* things are important is education and, believe it or not, that starts to sink in just about the time they are headed to college.

MAN UP Memos

- ✔ College is a place for students to learn to work without a net.
- ✔ They still need you and some rules in college.
- ✔ Colleges can be cesspools of human behavior.
- ✔ Make sure your kids understand and follow your expectations in college.

Attire

Recently, I was walking through a discount store and saw a six year-old little girl wearing hi-rise wedge shoes. Now, I don't know how many of you realize this but high heels and wedges are designed to flex the woman's calf so that they are shapely and will draw the male's attention. They also are extremely uncomfortable and there is a high risk of ankle injury (not to mention the effect on little growing feet).

Now, I assume that children should be children and should be able to run, jump and play. So, why on earth would anyone want to allow their little girl to wear shoes like that? Shoes that will hurt her feet, increase the likelihood of injury, and run the risk of developmental problems with her growing tootsies. Not to mention that there is no reason for attention to be drawn to a young girl's legs!

People, people, people, this is ludicrous! Economically speaking, most couples with young kids struggle to make ends meet. In many families, both parents work to provide for their families and then you see people buying junk like wedges for a six year old! And mind you, this was in a discount store! We are not talking about an upper end clientele here with lots of disposable income.

Children's clothing should be affordable, functional and age appropriate. They are going to grow or wear out clothes faster than you can imagine. When I was a young boy, my Mom would take a new pair of jeans, turn them inside out and sew patches in the knees before I ever wore them. She knew that I was going to wear holes in them faster than a wink.

When our kids were young, my wife's favorite store for clothes was a garage sale! There is no reason to spend lots of money on clothes that are going to be covered with smelly stuff for six months and then be too small to wear.

Children use their clothing differently than adults. Make sure that the clothing is appropriate. Wedge shoes on a six year-old girl are a great example of what not to do. A good pair of dress shoes and a good pair of sneakers is probably all your child will really need. Their feet grow faster than the rest of their bodies. So, you may as well contain your expenses by not pouring good money after bad.

Finally, let's talk about appropriate. Clothing lines today are selling you the label, not the quality of the goods. Just keep that in mind. Fads change and it is not a law that Mom and Dad have to pay hard earned wages for an Abercrombie shirt that looks like it was worn out fifteen years ago. If your child wants to wear stuff like that, tell them to get a job (or use their allowance if they have one). This way, they can spend their own money and learn the value of a hard-earned dollar.

Another aspect of appropriateness is the setting. There is nothing wrong with requiring your child to wear a button down or collared shirt to church. A teenager going to church wearing a Metallica T-shirt is just out of line. Parents, you have to control this; teach your children proper decorum. Hopefully, they wouldn't be meeting the President of the United States in holey jeans. So, holey jeans are not appropriate for holy places either.

Age and anatomy appropriateness is another thing. If you are blessed with teenage girls, just know this: at some point, they will want to flaunt their newfound forms. They just do. Dad, you aren't going to like it the first time your daughter dresses up in

"Daisy Dukes" and knee boots. You and your wife have to be aligned on what is and is not appropriate. You don't want to be arguing in front of the kids. So, get with Mom and get it settled first. If it looks like she is dressed to walk the streets, then MAN UP, draw a line in the sand and say NO.

MAN UP memos

- ✔ Children should not dress the same as adults.
- ✔ Don't waste money on clothing that is inappropriate or will be out grown quickly.
- ✔ Kids earning their own money for special clothes can be a teachable moment.

Video Games, the Internet, and Social Skills

Many of you will not realize the dramatic changes that have come about in our society over the last 30 years. When I was in high school, the home video game of choice was Pong, Michael Dell was in grade school and the Internet did not even exist.

During my work career, business has gone from face-to-face interaction and typed interdepartmental memos to real time global video-conferences from your laptop or cell phone. Many of our children spend more time interacting via Instant Messaging and texts than they do running and playing with their friends.

While the advent of the computer has electronically interconnected us, we are losing our ability to really connect as people. I can't tell you the number of times that, as a manager, I have received fuming emails from one employee to the next, ranting and raving about some inane topic. When I ask, "Have you spoken to him about it?" The answer was, "No, but I sent him an email."

When I see two people sitting 20 feet apart, and their primary means of communication is sending blurbs through the Internet, it makes me concerned whether our children are using a tool or if they are losing the ability to relate to other human beings.

We have to be very careful that our children are learning how to deal with people, with all of the warts and issues, with the joy and emotions, with the anger and problems. Without the ability to navigate through humanity, our children will be unprepared to build the emotional bonds, cope with the stresses of life and teach and train their own children how to do the same.

People don't recognize that when email or text is the primary means of communication, they are not really aware of the frame of mind of the recipient. Based on the theory of evolution, the human creature has been around for nearly 100,000 years. Language, as we know it, has only been around for about 10,000 years. The written word has only been around for about 5,000 years. Literacy of the masses has come about only in the last 100 to 200 years. These factoids mean that, for most of the period of human development, our communication was oral, visual and un-written.

Behavioral scientists tell us that humans have an uncanny adaptation wherein 90% of all communication is non-verbal. This means that 90% of the communication isn't what is said or written, but how it is stated or delivered. Body language, tone of voice, inflection and facial expression communicate more of the message than does the word itself. And, when the preferred means of communication is electronic, all of this messaging is lost.

When two people are communicating, the mood of the recipient determines the message received, not the mood of the sender.

Email arguments often start because the sender and receiver cannot tell the mood of the other. The sender sends text in one mood, and the receiver reads it in another mood. Without the sender and receiver knowing the state of mind of the other, things get disconnected.

The age of electronic communication is here. Video games are here. Just make sure that, like all other things, your child is balanced. Make sure that they have to spend time with others, learning appropriate social skills. Make sure that you monitor the content of their games and Internet sites. It is OK for you to set the rules, boundaries and yes, even curfew, on how and when your children are using electronic media.

MAN UP Memos

- ✔ Too much video and Internet is bad for social skill development.
- ✔ Be aware of the video, and music your children listen to.
- ✔ Curfews are an appropriate way to control media use.

Violence and Anger Management

A few weeks back, I was reading an article about a child, who had been raised by a Neo-Nazi. The boy was 10 years old and, for whatever reason, he had waited till his Dad had fallen asleep, took a gun and shot his father in the head, killing him instantly.

As the police were taking the boy away, the child asked the cop, "People get another life, don't they?" Most likely, this little boy had developed his thoughts on life and death from his exposure to video games and, tragically had assumed that his father would reboot and restart.

This story points out a couple of things. The first point ties to the previous chapter. Clearly, this child had a skewed sense of reality. Thinking that his Dad would get a restart, or a new life, is video game mentality. Our kids are thinking that, in life, they punch the button and get a replay. We have to teach them that this is not the case. They have to learn that there are serious repercussions in life.

The second and most troubling thing is the extreme violence to which this child had been exposed. Now you may think, "well this is just the case of a Neo-Nazi," but we see every single day situations in which violence is becoming more and more prevalent in society. We see situations regularly of abuse, we have set aside shelters to protect women and children, we see situations where bullying carried to an extreme, has caused someone to commit suicide.

In many of these instances, the perpetrator has learned a habit of violence, and the first teachers are ... Who else? The PARENTS. We have to teach our children that resorting to violence is not the way to handle stress or to deal with issues. We have to teach them that the most appropriate method for handling conflict is to talk through it or walk away from it.

As I mentioned in the chapter on discipline, I cautioned never to take a mode of discipline off the table and never to overuse a form of discipline. It is my belief that when a child is overexposed to corporal punishment, he is learning that violence is normal and acceptable. If a kid gets a swat for everything, sooner or later he will think it is OK to hand out swats, any time that things don't go his way.

I will tell you that, in some very rare cases, I believe that corporal punishment is appropriate. But, the emphasis is on VERY RARE. Our philosophy was that we did not apply corporal punishment unless the child's behavior was so severe that they were in danger or if they hurt or endangered someone else. By following this philosophy, a couple of things happen. First, your child will rarely cross over a line that puts him really in danger. Therefore, the frequency is automatically controlled. Second, by having such an infrequent punishment, the seriousness of the offense is emphasized and the child will, more than likely, know not to endanger himself or hurt another person.

Finally, we were always very controlled in the type of corporal punishment applied. A few open handed swats on the kiester is all that a kid should ever need to let them know that you are serious. And, if they know you will do it, the bluff is set. The better the bluff, the less likely you will ever have to use the punishment. Also realize that, as your kids get older, there are much more effective forms of discipline, anyway. Taking the car keys is much more effective on a teenager than a spanking!

Now, we just spent a bunch of time talking about violence but what really begets violence is uncontrolled anger. Let me tell you from experience, it is not possible to raise children without getting so angry that you can chew nails! You will be frustrated by their audacity, amazed at their ambivalence and stymied by their apparent lack of any form of common sense!

But remember: **their full time job is to press the buttons, to stretch the boundaries**. No matter how you see it as a parent, they are just doing what comes naturally. And whether you realize it or not, you did the same thing to your parents.

Now, this is where the anger management piece comes in. You have to teach them that you are in control. If you understand the roles, you know that they are, by nature, going to tick you off! But, by knowing that it will happen, you can prepare yourself to deal with it. You can set a standard of remaining in control. By controlling your own anger, you teach them to do the same thing.

I will tell you that with my Italian, German and Irish heritage this has probably been one of the biggest struggles of my life! I can also tell you that if someone had explained this to me when I was a young father, it probably would have kept my blood pressure lower over the years!

Don't forget the role of the child and try to keep your cool!

MAN UP Memos

- ✔ Society is increasingly more violent.
- ✔ You must teach your children violence and anger management.
- ✔ Understanding the roles of parents and kids will help you keep your cool.

SEXUALITY

You know, it is kind of funny that with all of the new thinking that has come about regarding sexuality over the last 40 years, this is probably the most difficult topic for parents to discuss with their kids.

Unfortunately, it is also the most important and potentially dangerous topic that our children will have to deal with. Sexuality, for both boys and girls, has the potential of disrupting their lives to an extent that few of us can imagine.

Parents have a tendency to not address the most serious aspects of sexuality and, as a result, our children are often ill prepared to deal with their sexuality as it blossoms during their teen years. They are also ill prepared to deal with the serious, long-term ramifications that sexuality can have on their lives.

To properly set up the discussion, I would like to start out with a series of facts:

- Today the average teenager becomes sexually active at the age of 14.
- Over 80 percent of the population has had intercourse before the age of 21.
- Approximately 40% of all children are born out of wedlock.
- Approximately 22% of all children conceived are aborted.

- Over 50% of women who have had abortions consider suicide.
- Over 40% have serious drug use.
- Over 50% of college students report sexual hookups with more than five partners.
- Attempted suicide is three times more likely for girls who are sexually active than for girls who are abstinent.
- 4% of youth between the ages of 18 and 26 have Chlamydia.
- 35% of women from 15 to 19 and 29% of women between 20 and 29 have HPV.
- HPV leads to genital warts, cervical cancer and complications for newborns.
- Chlamydia and HPV both can lead to infertility.
- Approximately 15% of childbearing couples in the US suffer from infertility.

These are some pretty staggering facts about what is occurring as a result of the "free sex" mentality and the sexual mores that have permeated our culture since the advent of the pill and the 1960's.

After learning that my wife was expecting our first child, I was at a wise old friend's house. I was explaining how thrilled we were. He asked me if I wanted a boy or a girl and, like a politically correct Dad, I said, "Really we don't have a preference, we just want it to be healthy." At this, my friend laughed and said "You, sir, are a ___ ___liar ... you want a boy, and I'll tell you why. With a boy, you only have to worry about one penis but with a girl, you have to worry about all of them!"

My friend laughed and went on about his business. But, he had unwittingly shared some pretty deep wisdom about our culture. We tend not to worry too much about our sons and worry a lot about our daughters. Our young women are the ones that bear the brunt of the issues when it comes to misplaced sexual behaviors. But, let me tell you something Dads; you have to teach your sons AND daughters. We cannot continue to condone a boy's sexual exploration as acceptable or normal, while we are putting our daughters at risk.

NEWS FLASH: "We are better than animals!" Sexual misconduct has become commonplace, but humans DO have the power to control their libido. We do not have to teach our children that sex with any one at any time is acceptable.

Those people we used to hold in high esteem often get a free pass and a shrug nowadays. From TV commercials, to movies, to sporting events, we have allowed behavior, dress and language to de-evolve. We are now at a point where our children are exposed to music every day that screams of group sex, oral sex, and anal sex. And parents aren't even aware that this is what their children are listening to.

Gentlemen, you have to wake up and smell the coffee. You cannot fight this affront to morality by platitudes and polite references of "faith, right and wrong, and saving yourself for the right one." You have got to get brutally honest! Talk to your kids bluntly and make sure that they know that bad things can and do happen to nice girls (and boys.)

At one time, every man wanted to make sure that the woman of his dreams was a virgin on their wedding night and that she was unspoiled and unshared. The problem is that today no one wants to keep them that way.

You have to teach your sons what is and is not acceptable and why. You have to teach your daughters and, quite frankly, you have to protect them. I used to hear that the best birth control was an aspirin, squeezed tightly between the knees. But with today's morality and the pervasiveness of alcohol, drugs, and an "anything goes" attitude, restraint on the girl's part just isn't enough.

Any Dad that would let his high school freshman daughter go out with a senior these days should have his head examined. A 15 year old is not prepared to deal with the pressure she will be under to succumb. She will also not be able to deal with the emotional distress that she will be subjected to when or if she does give in. You have to stand firm. It is not about trusting your child. It is about not trusting the kid that you don't know.

And, oh by the way, our society isn't helping you. New York City recently passed a law that forbids the sale of soft drinks in sizes greater than 20 ounces. On the same day, they passed a law that their public schools could give out the morning-after pill to underage girls without their parent's consent. This is the kind of mentality that we are dealing with. Being too fat is criminal but encouraging abortions and hiding it from the parents is ok.

Because of the degree of sexual misconduct in this country, we have aborted over 50 million children in the last 35 years. Our young women are dealing with the highest rates of sexually transmitted diseases in the nation's history. The rate of infertility is on the upswing and there is a rise in the number of sexual partners on both sides of the aisle.

What used to be called a tramp (male or female) is now becoming the norm. Dads, you have to look at your daughter and ask yourself, do you want your daughter to become a slut? If you don't like the sound of that, then you have to take a firm stand and do something about it. And, oh by the way, this is one of those areas where you won't be popular!

Your kids aren't going to like it when you put your foot down on clothing, who they hang out with, or on a curfew. Your answer needs to be "get over it." You aren't in a popularity contest. You are there to be a Dad and to give your children the best shot at a long and happy life. You have to MAN UP and shoulder the responsibility of disappointing them now, so they will be thankful when they are adults.

We used to say that the only difference between a slut and a prostitute was that a slut was free! Today, we are just calling her "liberated." Folks, if you haven't figured it out, **Free sex ain't free!** Our children and our grandchildren are paying for a failed experiment in free sexuality and in order to bring it under control you have to MAN UP. Teach your sons and daughters to be human and that SEXUAL SELF-CONTROL IS ONE OF THE THINGS THAT SETS HUMANS APART FROM THE ANIMALS.

One last area that needs to be discussed on sexuality is that of sexual predators. Gentlemen, they are out there. They are male and female, they are police, teachers, pastors, priests, aunts, uncles, cousins, parents and grandparents. You have the obligation to warn your children and prepare them. Teach them the difference between appropriate physical contact and inappropriate contact.

Watch your child's behavior. If you see a sudden shift, find out what is going on. Educate yourself so that you can better protect your kids. With the present state of our society, anytime that a child is in a situation where they are one-on-one with an adult, there can be risk. It doesn't matter who the adult is: pedophiles are very skilled at getting kids alone and making the parents feel that the child is safe.

You can't mistrust everyone but you do have to be careful. Learn and watch for the warning signs and, for gosh sake, make sure you have the sort of relationship with your kid that they will let you know if something happens that makes them uncomfortable. If your child is uncomfortable being around an adult, don't overlook their concern. Take the child's concern as a warning and look deeper into what is going on in your child's life.

MAN UP Memos

- ✔ Improper sexual behavior is hurting our kids.
- ✔ You must be able and willing to speak openly on this topic.
- ✔ Your kid's lives depend on it.

CHEMICALS

I was raised, in a time and a family, where the consumption of alcohol was pretty much common place. My Dad always told us, "If you want to drink, do it at home. You can have anything you want. Don't sneak around, just ask." Needless to say we snuck around, didn't ask, and went out drinking with our friends every chance we got. It is as if, regardless of the age limit or permissiveness of the parents, that a universal rite of passage is being able to buy alcohol while underage and not get caught.

Well boys, times have changed. Gone are the days when parents only worried about a kid sneaking a beer or smoking a cigarette. Gone are the days when a cop would let an intoxicated driver "go on home" as long as the traffic was light.

Today, fines and penalties can ruin a family. An MIP (minor in possession) can void a driver's license. Traffic and congestion is way up and so too, is the likelihood of an accident. An under the influence accident will get someone thrown under the jail. DUI doesn't mean under the influence, it means "legally over a blood level threshold" (that the kid cannot detect.) Today, there are more cheap drugs than at any point in our nation's history. And then, of course, there are the "date rape" drugs.

We had to teach our children not only to abstain from alcohol but also to never leave an open drink of any kind on the counter. They had to learn to only ride with or better yet to be the designated driver. We had to teach them that their entire future was at risk, if they went one drop too far.

We even had to teach our daughters to be aware while babysitting. There were a number of times, when they were not comfortable riding home with a "partying parent." We taught our girls that they were expected to call us and we would come and get them rather than allow an intoxicated adult to drive one of them home. There was more than one occasion when we were happy to get out of bed to go pick up our child because the parent was in no shape to be driving.

And oh, by the way, up until now we are just talking about the over-the-counter legal stuff. I mentioned earlier that New York was permitting schools to issue morning after pills to high school girls without their parent's knowledge.

Science is only beginning to understand the correlation between birth control pills and various women's cancers. And, there is growing evidence that the increase of birth control estrogen in the woman's body at the time of fetal development is having an adverse effect on male sexual development. There is additional evidence that residual levels of estrogen in the water supply may be affecting male sperm production.

Guys, our bodies were not designed to handle the wide range of chemicals that are now "FDA approved." Putting this stuff in our bodies is affecting the human species and frankly, there hasn't been enough time since the 1960's for all of the "new" developments to have been really vetted.

The point is, watch what is happening. And, don't start subjecting your kids to chemical cocktails any earlier than they have to be. Teach your children the difference between right and wrong, and don't let them depend on a pill to keep them out of trouble. Warn them about the things that they will see and be exposed to in junior high and high school.

While my daughter-in-law was pregnant with my first grandson, she never took a single pill or drop of alcohol. She was concerned about the health of the baby and about how much effect that just a "little bit" would have on a developing child. That is the kind of attitude that we need to embrace.

I can tell you that if kids were out running and playing and were getting a little more discipline at home, there would probably be a lot less need for Ritalin. Don't get me wrong: there are some children that really need it, but I would wager there are more parents that just need a good lesson in parenting than there are kids that need to be doped up! This is all about what is best for the child, not what is most expedient for Mommy and Daddy. Courage or cures from a bottle ain't all it's cracked up to be, especially for children!

One last note on chemicals; my father in law once took me to the place where he had attended grade school. He showed me the underground cistern where they captured the storm water runoff. He told me how they would put catfish in it to eat the mosquito larvae. He told me how the older boys would haul the water up in buckets and how all of the kids shared a single ladle to drink. I suspect that the first time he ever saw a doctor was when he was inducted into the military for WWII. My father-in-law lived to a ripe old age and could out work most men half his age.

The reason that I am telling this story is because it bothers me to see a kid go to the doctor every time he has a runny nose. Heck, when I was a kid we went to the doctor ... maybe once per year. With all the concern about the rising cost of health care, maybe we should be asking, "Does this child really need to go in for this?" If the fever isn't over 102, they'll usually get over it. If the limb moves, it's probably not broken. If the blood isn't spurting out, they won't bleed to death. And for gosh sakes, you don't need antibiotics for every sniffle! Sometimes it is better to just let nature run the course and allow them to build up a little immunity. The point here is to be reasonable.

Just keep the prescribed stuff balanced and warn your kids about the legal and illegal drugs that they will be exposed to. Drugs are one of those topics for repetitive communication. The exposure is so great and the risks are so extreme that you owe it to your children to prepare them. This will be one of those really uncomfortable areas, but you all know someone that has had their life turned upside down due to chemicals. Make sure it doesn't happen to your own child.

MAN UP Memos

- ✔ Legal and illegal chemicals are having negative effects on our health.
- ✔ Educate yourself and your kids on chemical use and abuse.
- ✔ Not all that the Dr. allows is good for you.

Porn

What? Why the heck is he writing a chapter on porn? There, I've said it for you. So, listen up! Remember all of those commandments I wrote about earlier? One of them had to do with lusting after your neighbor's wife. Oh, yeah... Well, there really are problems that arise from porn. It is affecting our families and our kids.

We've already talked about the divorce rate hovering near 50%. A recent US study showed that nearly half of all divorced couples state that porn is a major reason for the break up. If you do the math, that means that nearly 25% of all married couples divorce due to the effects of pornography.

What's more, over 70% of males between the ages of 18 and 34 have visited porn websites, 55% of hotel movie rentals are for porn, 47% of all families report porn problems and 33% of all companies have terminated employees for using porn on the job.

And, without getting into some pretty serious physiology, the human body chemically reacts in such a way that pornography is actually addictive. Due to the chemicals that your brain releases while viewing porn and during climax, the human body can actually become addicted to porn.

Women on the other hand deal with a couple of aspects. What woman would not be disturbed to find out that her husband is more turned on by the woman on the screen, than by his own wife? As a result of their husbands' use of porn, many wives become depressed and the marital satisfaction with each other is severely impacted.

Furthermore, there is the pain and agony of the men and women engaged in the porn industry. Every one of those girls on parade has a Daddy. Most of them are lured into the industry by dreams of fame and fortune and the vast majority of them end up rejected by friends, family or abused by people in the industry.

With today's access to the Internet, kids are being exposed to porn at an earlier and earlier age and, unlike the soaps you see on TV, what is happening on the porn screen isn't acting. It is real sexual activity. Activity that is repetitively performed so many times just to catch the right scene, that often the women are threatened or abused to the point of tears.

The creation of porn is humanity at its worst and viewing porn only drives the demand for a horrid industry. Furthermore, the industry is so attuned to its addictive nature that they are intentionally targeting our children in order to sustain business growth.

When I was growing up, the only way for boys to get access to porn was to find a magazine, get an adult to buy it, or flip through the lingerie ads in the women's magazine and conjure it up! Today, hard-core porn is accessible to anyone who has access to the Internet or a cell phone. This stuff can be in your house, car or your kid's bedroom without you ever knowing it.

Dads, you have to be aware of what your children/teens are viewing and which websites they are hitting. Put the computer in a room where they can't hide the sites they are visiting. And for Pete's sake, NEVER think that this is a victimless crime. Think of those girls on the screen and ask, "Do you want your daughter doing that?" If the answer is no, then take porn seriously and make sure that your sons and daughters are protected.

One last thing: your kids aren't going to like you very much when you check out their browser history or IPOD listings. The debate will start, you can reason all you want, they will never like it, so the eventual answer is "Get over it." The sooner you get there, the less yelling and frustration there will be, and the sooner they'll actually "get over it."

MAN UP Memos

- ✔ Pornography is destroying 25% of the marriages in America.
- ✔ Porn is a serious issue among both boys and girls.
- ✔ No parent wants their kids to grow up to be porn stars.
- ✔ Monitor your kid's music, books and Internet sites.

DEADBEAT DADS

Deadbeat Dads really get under my skin. These are the guys that you hear about fathering a child and then disappearing. Refusing to provide support for their wife and children, financial or otherwise. These are the guys that always have something better to do than spend time with their kids. These are the guys that refuse to consider that they have an obligation to fulfill, because they are responsible for bringing that young life into this world.

The problem is that at one point in time or another, pretty much all of us are deadbeats, at least for a little while. From the guy who spends too much time at work, to the guy who is locked into the web, to the guy who spends so much time doing charitable work that he forgets about his family.

We are all deadbeats at one point in time or another. When your child walks through the room and says "Hi Dad!" and you don't look up from the paper ... yep, you guessed it. Deadbeat. When your wife is pulling out her hair because the kids have been holy terrors and you aren't receptive to helping her ... yep, you guessed it. Deadbeat. And yes, when you leave your wife and family and chase the skirt that sits two offices down ... BIG DEADBEAT.

Men, you were there when that family was created. You were there when that little life was created. You were the one that said, "Till death do us part." I have never heard a vow that said, "Till I see something better."

Our society must get back to the point where we mean what we say and we live up to our vows and promises. If a man won't live up to his promise to his own wife and family, then why on earth would we expect him to live up to a contract in a business environment?

In my opinion, there ain't no such thing as "irreconcilable differences." There are men that are failing to live up to their commitment. There are women failing to live up to their commitment. There is a failing of the couple to work hard enough to make things work. We have to start speaking the truth and get to the bottom line if we are going to start turning around the fabric of our society.

Now, a lot of you may think that I have just gone off my rocker. But the fact is, the only way for a child to learn the right way to live is if he has a positive family role model. The only way he gets that is if his Mom and Dad are there, living out their vows and working out their differences to make the family unit strong.

We owe it to the next generation to provide a better foundation than the one that we received and the only way to do that is for Moms and Dads to work together to strengthen the family. They have to set aside their differences, fix the weak spots and build on the strengths that each parent possesses.

This is how you build a family and that's what this book is all about, teaching each of you how to improve on your own capabilities as a Dad. So listen up and MAN UP.

MAN UP Memos

- ✔ All Dads are Deadbeat Dads at some point.
- ✔ You can have a good job, good wages, live at home and still be a deadbeat Dad.
- ✔ It's never too late to turn around.

Recovering Deadbeats

One of the greatest gifts that God ever gave us is the fact that our children love us. It is absolutely amazing that in spite of all our errors, issues, problems, mistakes and fits of anger, they still love us and will forgive us. A child can truly teach us a lot if we will only let them. So take heart, men, even if (or when) you have been a Deadbeat Dad, it is still not too late to redeem yourself!

Over the last few years, I have watched a TV program that has followed a father and son who started out as business partners. Over the years, their relationship has fallen apart primarily as a result of extraordinarily poor and domineering behavior on the father's part. As time moved on, the family and business was torn apart and now, slowly, after four years, the two have started to patch up their differences.

To me, this is really a testimony to the strength of love and forgiveness. All that it took to begin to rebuild the relationship is for each man to recognize that they had both made mistakes, that they each wanted to change and they were each willing to apologize.

The best possible thing that a Deadbeat Dad should know is that the vast majority of kids are willing to forgive. **But it will take effort on the Father's part.** You have to recognize that you aren't perfect. You have to be willing to apologize and you have to be willing to show your love for the child.

I guarantee you; until you are gone from this world it is never too late to hug your son or daughter. It is never too late to tell them that you love them and that you are proud of them. This is all that most kids really want from their Dad: to know that they are loved. It is so typical for a man to hold back his love and affection. It is hard for a lot of men to express the way that they feel and, as a result, kids are often left wondering if their Dads had really cared for them. Dads, you have to change that while you still have the time to do so.

There is something that is happening today, socially, that has the potential to really help this happen: The Man-Hug. When you see two friends, who are capable of giving each other a bear hug, then we aren't far away from a father and son being able to share a hug as well.

When I was about ten, I remember telling my Dad, "Aww Dad, boys don't hug each other." I regret that I ever spoke these words to him and wish now that I had more Daddy hugs. This is something that I have always cherished with my own kids. My son and daughters are all grown, out of the house and starting their own families. But we still give each other those big old hugs every time we can!

Recovering Deadbeats, there is a lot of healing in a hug. Remember that!

MAN UP Memos

- ✔ Admitting when you are wrong is a good thing.
- ✔ Teaching forgiveness is a better thing.
- ✔ There is a lot of healing in a HUG.

Other People's Kids (Including Grandkids)

One of the interesting things about being a Dad is that every now and then you have the opportunity to be a Dad to someone else's kids. Whether you are a coach, teacher, scout leader, uncle, grampa, or your kids are just having an overnight sleep-over--just for a short period of time, you are being entrusted with the life of someone else's precious child.

So the question is ... how do you do this? And the answer is to treat them as if they are your own. Now let's face it: you may not be able to ground or provide a much-needed paddling to someone else's kid. But other than that, you can pretty much expect anyone under your care to act the same way you would expect your own child to act.

That means there is nothing wrong with expecting a guest in your home to act with respect, pull their own weight and live according to the rules of the house.

One time, my daughter had a friend over to spend the night. They were teenagers and my wife and I expected an evening of giggling and girl stuff. Well, about 9:30 I asked where Sally was and my daughter replied that Sally was out on a walk ... after dark ... with her boyfriend, who had quietly showed up, unannounced. Sally had left without permission and here I was, with a missing teenager.

After a few more questions, I found out that Sally's folks were not big fans of the boyfriend and that she had asked him over so she could be with him without her parents knowing. Well, needless to say, I almost went ballistic and then just waited for the two to return. When Sally tried to sneak back in, I politely invited her and her would-be suitor into the living room and proceeded to share with him a little "fatherly advice." I explained to him that her Daddy had placed her in my hands, just like a little chick. And, like a big old yard dog, it was my job to protect her and I would do so, at all cost. And, this young man would not stand in the way of me accomplishing that task. When he took her out of my home without my knowledge, he endangered her and he had violated my responsibility to protect her.

I once heard that stress is defined as, "The confusion created when one's mind overrides the body's desire to beat the snot out of someone who desperately needs it."

Let's just say that I was under stress, but as polite as possible — under the circumstances. By the end of the evening, they both knew that in my world, they played by my rules. They also knew that if her Daddy would not approve, I certainly did not approve, either!

Something that surprised me about the episode was my daughters' reaction. While I was sure that my daughter would be upset, instead, she was quite happy about the outcome! She later confided that she was concerned about Sally the whole time she had been gone and was glad that I had taken care of her.

There is absolutely nothing wrong with being a strong Dad to anyone with whom you have been entrusted. To this day, my daughter and Sally laugh about the time that I "took care" of Sally. They even quote the "little chick" line. In that one instance, I showed Sally how much that a Dad can love their child and how a father's love can spill over to others, as well.

And by the way, that goes for Grampa's too. Now, I don't have any practical experience as a Grampa just yet, but I have seen a lot of really good Grampas. And the ones that are the best are the ones that are really good Dads. They show their grandchildren that while they are loved, they still need to play by the rules set by Mommy and Daddy.

Now Grampas: Mommy and Daddy set the rules in their own home. And Mommy and Daddy have the final say so on how the kids will be raised. The parents have the right to raise their children according to their own set of rules. However, I have seen a lot of situations where the parents fail to keep the kids under control in Grampa's house and Grampa just knuckles under.

That, my friend's, is pure HOGWASH! It is perfectly acceptable to expect your adult children to control their own children while visiting your home. Under their roof, their rules apply. But at your house, by gosh, you still pay the bills! Don't embarrass your kids, by any means, but it is still your house and you and Grandma still deserve respect.

By expecting your children and grandchildren to respect your space as grandparents and continuing to show all of them the love that they deserve, you will have the opportunity to continue to demonstrate what a great Dad you were ... and still are. And your kids and grandkids will love you for it!

MAN UP Memos

- ✔ You can be a Dad to other people's kids.
- ✔ With the exception of discipline, treat them as your own.
- ✔ The love of a good Dad will spill over to your kid's friends.

Working Through the Crisis

When I was ten years old, my older brother was killed in Vietnam. This was a crisis for my family that my parents were not prepared to deal with. So, as most parents did back then, they just had to muddle through. They did the best that they knew to do. This was before the time of support groups and Google searches. They struggled with pain and guilt. They asked why God would allow this terrible thing to happen. Each of them dealt with it in their own way and my siblings and I each dealt with it alone, as well. Our family was affected terribly as a result of this tragedy and there are still after-effects today.

The point of this chapter is to realize that crises are going to happen. They happen to everyone. Pain is a part of life, whether it is a death in the family or a terrible illness, the loss of job or a divorce, an assault on a family member or a child coming out of the closet. These sorts of events can and do happen to every family. And, in every family, it is up to Mom and Dad to lead them through the tough times.

The first thing to remember, in times of crisis, is that you are not alone. You are the head of a family. As such, you have to keep the family in mind. When my brother was killed, my Dad's reaction was private and to himself. We never knew what he was thinking, nor were we ever able to see his emotions. The problem with this approach was that he never acknowledged the turmoil to the rest of the family. By his own solitude, he put the family in a mode of dealing with the loss as individuals.

As a Dad, you have to recognize that your family needs you. They obviously will depend on you for your strength but they also need you to be human. They need to see a healthy way of dealing with the stress and the pain. They need to see a positive example of how to deal with a bad situation.

When bad things happen, people often ask, "How can a good God allow such terrible things to occur?" The only answer that I have ever heard that makes sense is, "so a greater good can come about." Essentially, bad things occur, but you can enable good to grow out of them. When you see someone with cancer, it is a terrible tragedy. But, when you see the outpouring of love and affection that takes place and the lives that are changed, good often occurs as well. If you recall what happened across the nation after 9/11; the outpouring of love, of patriotism and of community helped the entire nation to deal with the tragedy of that terrible day.

It is not possible to prevent bad things from happening. All that we can do is handle the bad things in a positive manner. We can either allow the bad to destroy our family or we can figure out ways to enable something positive. There are countless stories of how parents have taken the tragedy of a lost or injured child and turned it into something good. When times are tough, just realize that your family is looking to you to set things straight.

Life is not about preventing all of the bad things from occurring. That is just not possible. All that we can control is how we deal with good or bad when it happens. It is possible to take a seemingly good event (like a new job or promotion) and turn it into something terrible for the family (like Dad spending way too much time on the job, eventually putting pressure on the family.)

It is also possible to take a bad event and turn it into something positive, like the mother that founded MADD after her child was killed in an auto accident. The fact is that life is about playing the cards that you are dealt. By focusing on how you can turn any situation into something positive, with love and affection, you are preparing your child to reap the best out of life.

I have often been amazed at how children cope with illness. My little nephew has a condition that makes him susceptible to broken bones. He is required to undergo treatments once a quarter that are painful and make him ill. As a tiny child, he just weathers the treatment and the pain, and moves on with life. He doesn't see himself differently than other kids and is the happiest, sweetest little boy you would ever imagine!

His innocence and loving nature make him a role model, not only for other children, but for Dads as well. If a little child can take on such a difficult situation with such grace and peace, then this is a model that Dads can learn from and emulate. Your family is looking to you for strength and emotional support. Grace and peace in the face of difficult situations is a wonderful model for your kids!

MAN UP Memos

- ✔ Every family will deal with crisis.
- ✔ Your family needs you when crises occur.
- ✔ It's not the cards you are dealt; it's how you play them.

What Happens When Being a Good Dad Just Isn't Enough?

A friend of mine is one of the most loving, caring men I have ever known. He has four kids and he and his wife have done everything they could for their family. They have had wonderful times as a family but have struggled through pain, as well. As I have watched him over the years, one of the things that I have admired is his patience.

One of his children, in spite of all of the coaching and parenting, has wandered a long way from where his parents would prefer. He just hasn't responded to all of the guidance and love that his Mom and Dad have shared with him. In fact, the more they have cared, the further astray the child has gone. The further off course that this child has gone, the more patient the Dad has become. He has never lost his faith in the child, but he has given him space.

Sometimes, for whatever reason, a child just chooses a path that diverges from where his parents would prefer. Maybe it is due to bad relationships, or chemicals, personality or even a career track, but the child just doesn't respond to guidance. So, what is a parent to do?

First of all, you have to accept the fact that your children are going to grow up. At some point they have free will. You cannot govern their movements nor force their decisions. You have done all you can by the time they are out of high school or college. After that, you have to allow them to live their own lives.

You also have to recognize that you will always want the best for your kids, but that just isn't how life works. Some will do better than others. Sometimes, they will make bad choices and sometimes they will be the victims of circumstance. All that you can do is to teach, guide and prepare your child to deal with life. But Dads, you (and Moms) have to let your kids live out their own lives. Just as a coach stands on the sidelines and watches the game, you as parents, have to do the same thing. As painful as it may be, you have to let the kid's play the game.

As parents, you will always love your child. They are a part of you. However, that does not mean that you have to accept the decisions or the behaviors. You have heard the term: "hate the sin but love the sinner." As a parent, you will see your child make mistakes or bad decisions. You don't have to condone the behavior, nor do you have to bend your rules to accommodate them. But, always make sure they know you love them, regardless of the situation.

Finally, rest assured that you have done the best job that you knew to do. If you believe you did a better job as a Dad than your own father, you've done your best! There aren't any direction manuals that come with your kids (of course, most men wouldn't read the directions anyway.) The fact is that, as a parent, you have had to manage by guidelines, facing each application based upon the child and situation.

There are no "cut and dried" right answers. All you can do is your best, given your philosophy, your spouse, your child and the situation. Being a Dad is more art than science, so once you have done your best, kick back, have a cold one and trust that in the long run your kid will be OK.

Always be patient. Kids are humans. As such, they are pretty unpredictable. It may take years for them to come around but, sooner or later, the odds are that they will appreciate what you did for them and that you did the best you could. Who knows ... maybe one day your child will even write a book to share with others the things he remembered from you!

Finally, if you really think you have screwed up, ask for forgiveness from your kids, from your spouse and learn to forgive yourself. The only time it is too late to be a good Dad is once you are "toes up." As long as you can let your family know that you love them and that you are sorry for any mistakes that you have made, there is always a chance for forgiveness.

The only way that forgiveness can occur is to begin by asking for it. In the Lord's Prayer, Christians ask God to "forgive us our sins as we forgive those who sin against us." This means that we can only expect forgiveness to the same degree that we are willing to give it away.

So, whether the hurt is from you to others or from others to you, acknowledge the mistakes and make sure that the healing of forgiveness can take place. As leader of the family you have to LEAD. A real leader does not ask others to do what they are unwilling to do themselves.

And for Pete's sake, don't be one of those idiots with so much pride that they sit around waiting for the other person to make the first move. If you didn't teach your child to apologize first, then they probably won't. Life is too short to wait for the other person to make the first move. So MAN UP, acknowledge your faults and begin to repair any issues that may exist!

MAN UP Memos

- ✔ There is no such thing as a perfect Dad or perfect children.
- ✔ Even great Dads have problem children.
- ✔ Children have free will to follow their own path as adults.
- ✔ If you did your best, that's all you can do.
- ✔ Never be afraid to apologize.

Preparing the Next Generation of Dads

Over the years, I have had literally hundreds of conversations with my son, son-in-law, other fathers and men of all ages on the topics in this book. Of course, my son and daughters received some first-hand knowledge on how to raise kids, (whether they liked it or not!) And while my wife and I would probably use different words to describe our child-rearing methods, we have aligned very well in practice over the years.

You don't really think much about teaching your children how to parent while you are raising them. Instead, you are thinking about preparing the meal, going to work, paying the bills and worrying about paying for college. But the fact is that **your actions are teaching your kids how to parent**, every step of the way.

What you condone, they will condone. The behaviors you demonstrate, they will most likely demonstrate. The rules you make, will most likely become the rules that they use for their own kids.

There was a song years ago called, "Cat's in the Cradle." In it, the singer traces the growth of a young boy to adulthood. In each verse, the boy wants to spend time with his Dad and the Dad always has something else to do. But the refrain is always a loving, "I'm gonna be like you, Dad." At the end of the song, the Dad has retired and wants to spend time with the adult son, who now has a family and job of his own. The young man no longer has time to spend with his Dad. The final refrain is the Dad recognizing that "My boy was just like me."

I can never listen to that song because it reminds me of how fleeting life is, as is the time that we have with our family. My children are grown and live a long distance from us. As I write this, my daughter-in-law is expecting our first grandchild any day. A grandchild that will be raised 1500 miles away. I ask myself: Did I really do enough to teach my son how to be a good Dad? Does he recognize the good, so he can build on it? Does he recognize the bad, so he can improve upon it? Will he be a better Dad for my grandchildren than I was for him?

I have the same thoughts about my sons-in-law. The one I have and the one that my daughter hasn't yet met. I wonder: What did their Dads teach them? Did they learn to be good Dads? What were their role models like? Will they do a better job for my grandkids than their Dads did for them?

For millennia, being a Dad was passed down from father to son. There weren't books, only stories. There weren't classes, only learn-by-the-ropes. The training ground was years of following your Dad around, learning by his example. And, for better or worse, it was this method of Man-to-Man training that has allowed our species to make it this far.

Now, there is a totally new paradigm. Single-parent families are unfortunately the norm. The nuclear family is changing before our very eyes and in a time window too rapid for evolution. The only way that we can prepare the next generation of Dads is to speak man-to-man, to hope and pray that with books and classes, we can make up for all the Dads that have been missing-in-action over the last two generations. And, we have to repair a lot of damage done by social experiments launched over the last 50 years.

Generations of local knowledge are slipping away and the results of that loss are showing up in our courtrooms and jails all over the country. We have to stem the tide or we, like so many successful nations before us, will fall into history's heap of cultures that have risen and then fallen into ruin.

We each have a responsibility to pass on, to the next generation, the best knowledge and advice that we have to offer. This is my attempt at helping to pass on the collective wisdom of the hundreds of successful fathers that I have come to know over the years.

MAN UP Memos

- ✔ Your children will follow the pattern that you set.
- ✔ Your responsibility is to teach them what a good Dad is.
- ✔ Help teach other men to be good Dads as well.

PAY IT FORWARD

Well guys ... That's all I have. I have shared with you the techniques and thoughts that have been shared with me by my father and grandfathers, by my friends who have been successful and those who have struggled. I have tried to make the book direct, thought provoking, humorous and serious when it needed to be.

I cannot begin to claim that I have practiced all that I have preached. While I have done my best, every day I think about something that I did wrong or I failed to do. The Lord knows that there are situations I would recall and relive, if it were only possible.

One of the things that I have learned is that it is nearly impossible to repay your mentors for all of the gifts that they have given you. In business and in life, you will receive wisdom from those whom you will never be able to repay.

This is why we need to PAY IT FORWARD. Each of us has the responsibility of mentoring those who follow behind us. Not only to prepare our own children but to also help those who have not had the benefit of a stable family. If you can embrace even some of the concepts and thoughts of this book, and incorporate them into your own family, your kids and grandkids will have the opportunity to reap the benefits. If you can share this book and its thoughts with other men, then you have the ability to have a broader impact on a bunch of children that really need a good Dad.

The concepts are simple, but you will struggle with them every day. Your kids will look at you like you are a three-headed monster but, one day, after they are grown and they have kids of their own, they will come back and thank you.

Many of these thoughts seem to be common sense. But, to some men, they will be as foreign as a new language. Being a good Dad doesn't come naturally to everyone, but it is something that I believe every man can learn.

This book stemmed from talking man-to-man. So, if you value what you have learned, all I can ask is that you MAN UP and PAY IT FORWARD.

MAN UP Memos

- ✔ You can never repay your mentors.
- ✔ You can pass it on to the next generation.
- ✔ PAY IT FORWARD!

www.manupthebook.com